Praise for *The Fun Master*

T0046806

"Jeff Seitzer writes beautifully about the love between parent and child. You will laugh, cry, and ultimately understand why children are our greatest teachers. Above all, this moving memoir honors his son's incredible impact on everyone he met."

—Nadine Kenney Johnstone, author of *Of This Much I Am Sure*

"If life is learning, Jeff Seitzer is uniquely equipped. Bringing to bear his philosophical voice on the minutiae of raising a child with special needs, Seitzer has created a memoir as self-effacing as it is fearlessly honest."

—Sarah Terez Rosenblum, author of *Herself When She's Missing*

"Beautifully told and deeply moving—a gripping tale about infinite joy and sadness alike, and about the ironies that life contains. It takes a powerful writer like Seitzer to treat these ironies with the right mix of involvement, distance, and wonder, and to show the impossible— namely, how to reconcile the unreconcilable."

—Rainer Forst, winner of the Leibniz Prize
and author of *Toleration in Conflict*

"Jeff Seitzer has penned a beautiful memoir detailing the struggles of a father with CMT. I found this book funny, inspiring, and full of love. I hope he writes many more! "

—Clark Semmes, author of *The Tribe of Thin Ankles*

The Fun Master

The Fun Master

A Father's Journey of Love, Loss, and Learning to Live One Day at a Time

Jeff Seitzer

Published by SparkPress, a BookSparks imprint,
A division of SparkPoint Studio, LLC
Phoenix, Arizona, USA, 85007
www.gosparkpress.com

Published 2022
Printed in the United States of America
Print ISBN: 978-1-68463-149-0
E-ISBN: 978-1-68463-150-6
Library of Congress Control Number: 2022903574

Formatting by Kiran Spees

To Ethan, for changing my life.
To Penelope, for saving my life.
And to Janet, for just about everything.

Werewolves on TV.
My dad lets me watch the show.
I'm very happy.

Ethan McGinnis Seitzer
September 3, 2000–August 16, 2010

Contents

1 My Writing Assignment

I COASTED UNDER THE metal archway of the resort's entrance and pedaled down its circular drive, enjoying the sound of gravel crunching and popping under my tires. After I put the groceries away and added more ice to Janet's drink, I set up a yoga mat on the front porch of our quaint yellow cottage. Just as I positioned myself in a down-dog pose, Ethan arrived.

"Hi, Dad!" he said, setting up underneath me in the opposite direction so that we made eye contact.

"You know, Ethan, it looks like your head is attached to your bum."

He laughed his throaty laugh. "Too bad Penelope isn't here. We could do a triple," he said, prompting me to smile about the three of us doing yoga, fitting together like a set of human Tupperware.

I sat down on the mat facing him. "Where are the girls?"

"Mom, Penelope, and I went down to see the Grand Canyon," he said, referring to the large hole in the sand some teenage boys had dug the day before. "The Otts came by. They all want to go swimming. Mom said I can only go if you're with me."

I glanced out the window at the lake and sighed. The plan was to play mini golf because of Ethan's sunburn from the day before. A loud thud on the roof, followed by the scratching sounds of a squirrel

1

scurrying away with a prized acorn, drew our attention, giving me a moment to think. Skin cancer wasn't an abstraction to me, something only strangers experienced. My mom died of melanoma at fifty-seven, five years older than I was. My good friend Doug befell the same fate nine years ago. We took nine-month-old Ethan to his funeral. Really, though, what were the chances of Ethan contracting skin cancer from one sunburn?

Ethan's pleading interrupted my musings. "Come on, Dad. We can beat my record."

"Oh, buddy," I said, with a laugh meant to conceal how seriously I took records kids made up. Ethan's persistence reminded me of one from my childhood that I still longed to best. Steps from where I grew up in Omaha, there were two very large public parks separated by a major thoroughfare. A creek ran all the way along one edge of each park and underneath the busy six-lane street through a system of tunnels, all very dark, dank, and slimy, which made them truly irresistible. The tunnels forked at various points, and icky green liquid oozed out of openings near the rounded ceilings and down the walls. We explored them all, on foot or on bikes, often a bunch of dogs at our sides barking furiously. "NO TRESSPASSING" and "DANGER/ KEEP OUT" signs everywhere? That is but to laugh! We were down there every chance we got trying to break the "world record for the distance traveled without a light in a dark tunnel," until those killjoys at the parks department closed off the entrance.

Ethan's determination to break "the world record for the longest time jumping in the waves" made me so uncomfortable because I completely understood why it was so important to him.

The hardest part of parenting for me was the hypocrisy of refusing your kids the very things you wanted at their age. I had long since come to terms with the routine boredom and not doing what *I* really wanted to do much of the time. But the hypocrisy so essential to effective parenting wore away at my spirit. Resigned to always feeling bad about saying no most of the time, I strove to at least not get mad at them for asking me for something that I was duty bound to deny them. It was their job as kids to ask and my job as a parent to say no.

Working very hard to stay in character, to appear sympathetic but firm, I answered, "I don't know, buddy. We're worried about your sunburn. Goofing around at Captain Mike's with Penelope all day will be a blast, don't you think?"

Failure! There I was, pleading, not being firm. I showed an opening, encouraging negotiation. I knew that not allowing Ethan to swim in the noonday sun was the right choice. But his enthusiasm worked on me like pheromones, softening my resolve.

I shifted my gaze to avoid eye contact. Ethan broke the silence.

"Hello, Dad? Are you in there?"

"You can show Penelope all the fun stuff there, like the little boats," I said.

"Sure," he responded. "Of course, we cannnn do that after we swim."

I forced a smile and I recalled what a rush it had been to frolic in the waves the day before. After a deep breath, I nodded, prompting him to jump up and whoop with joy. He did a little dance with his arms extended.

"Put your swimsuit on, and I'll be down soon."

He swept a hand across his midsection like one of the models on an old game show, drawing the audience's attention to a prize.

"Oh," I said with a smile, realizing he spent his entire summer in baggy swimsuits.

He scampered to the door and stopped suddenly. "Hey, look. I set up Penelope's action figures."

I scanned the array. Cinderella, Sleeping Beauty, the evil stepsisters, King Henry, the fairy sisters, Quasimodo, and Esmeralda.

"We're only missing the handsome prince," he said. His eyes widened when he noticed the decaf iced mocha. "Can I have a sip?"

I nodded. He smiled and disappeared out the door with the drink. "Hey, that's for your mom, you know!" I shouted after him.

I put on a swimsuit, gathered up some snacks, towels, and sunscreen, and walked out the door. Descending the steep stairs to the beach, I regretted not taking the time to pack everything more carefully. Each step loosened my grip on one thing or another until a tube of sunscreen worked its way loose and did a cartwheel before resting at the edge of the stairs. I flashed it an angry glance, then scanned the beach for the fallen tree near the water's edge where I knew the so-called Grand Canyon was. After noting the best way to it, I grabbed the sunscreen, picked up the rest of the stuff, and continued down the stairs.

I trudged across the sand and paused to let a gaggle of kids pass. I took the opportunity to reassert my authority over the uncooperative beach accessories. I hadn't gotten far when I was startled to hear someone yell, "Incoming!" I turned to my right just as a Nerf football landed on the bunch of towels that balanced atop the picnic basket wedged precariously between my forearms. A young man with a big smile grabbed it, apologized, and ran off down the beach.

I saw Janet at the edge of the canyon, radiant as always. Her beautiful red hair shimmered in the bright sunshine. Hearing her laughter harmonize with the excited chatter of the kids made me smile, charmed by the prospect of a great week at the beach.

Suddenly, Ethan's head popped up just above ground level. Two of the Ott kids, Sergio and Rosa, and Olivia and Abbey, the daughters of friends also vacationing in the area, then climbed over the edge like soldiers out of a World War I foxhole and ran off to a nearby puddle. Ethan boosted Penelope up out of the pit, and the two of them joined the other kids.

I hugged Janet and kissed her forehead; we stood arm in arm watching the kids play. "While you were shopping, we came down to play on the beach. Steve and the kids arrived and assumed we planned to swim. I know we weren't going to swim," she said. "But everyone else is going in, and Ethan begged me, on bended knee no less."

I nodded, put everything down, and gazed out at the lake. "It's kinda hard to resist swimming today, I have to admit. It's just so beautiful."

When Steve arrived with swimsuits, Janet took the kids except Ethan to change. Steve padded down the beach, and I began reading. Ethan soon joined me.

The crests of the waves were brilliant white in the bright August sun. It was hypnotic watching the water deposit swimmers gently near shore. I snapped out of my trance when a college-aged boy a few feet to our left was knocked onto his back and disappeared under the water except for his lower legs. The water rushed back out over him, and he sat up coughing. Ethan and I glanced at one another, then directed our gaze back at him, both breathing a sigh of relief when he broke out in uproarious laughter.

Two of his friends rushed over to help him up. "That was great!" he exclaimed, causing me to chuckle.

Is that all you got? I imagined him saying to the mythical god of the lake.

His chums enthusiastically nodded their assent. "Let's go!" one of them shouted. They ran high-kneed out into the surf with their arms wrapped around each other's shoulders.

Ethan turned toward me. "Can we go in the water now?"

"Let's wait until the others get here."

"Okay," he said, disappointed, then asked, "What are you reading?"

"*The Iliad*. I'm teaching it this fall."

"Cool. That's about Achilles and the Trojan War, right?"

I nodded with a smile. Ethan had written a poem the year before about wanting to meet Achilles. At the time, I'd wondered how he knew about him. But earlier in the summer he had seen me flipping through Edith Hamilton's *Mythology* and said he'd like to read it again. I had forgotten that he'd read some of it while waiting for a doctor's appointment after we had left his book in the car.

"We should read it together this fall."

"Great," he said as Abbey sat down next to him. They began talking while I glanced over to see Janet and Steve chatting and the other kids chasing Penelope. As I rose to talk to Janet about how the day would go, Ethan sprang up and ran into the waves, leaving his hearing aids squeaking at my feet. I sighed, turned off his hearing aids, and stowed them in my bag.

Abbey turned to me and asked, "Should he be in the water by himself?"

"No, he shouldn't," I said, feeling anxious that Janet and I hadn't had a chance to talk about safety precautions. "Into the breach once more," I added as I hustled in after him with Steve and the other kids close behind.

Ethan and I joined a long line of wave crashers extending in both directions about twenty feet from shore, where the water was less than two feet deep. The water level rose as the first wave washed past us, forcing us back a bit. That signaled the approach of a much bigger wave. We looked at one another and then at the others and braced ourselves, brimming with excitement. As if responding to a telepathic command, we dived forward in unison into the center of the big wave, which lifted all of us back to shore, leaving everyone on their bums, laughing, in a few inches of water.

Because of the direction of the waves and configuration of the shoreline, we ended up far down the beach from where we'd started. Groups of revelers ran back to their starting points and began the process over again. After about an hour, I stopped Ethan during one of these resets to check his sunburn. "Isn't this great? I'm going to beat my record."

"I'm not sure about that, buddy," I said, trying to apply more sunscreen. "I think we may go just a couple more times."

"Okay," he said, beaming.

His enthusiasm was infectious. I had become carried away with the thrill of diving into the waves and lost track of Steve and the others. Hearing people all around us, I assumed they weren't far away. I swam a bit farther out in hopes of riding a bigger wave back, then heard Ethan scream.

"I don't like it when you're so far away from me. I'm serious, Dad. Daaaddd!"

A wave crashed into my face. Coughing, struggling to stay afloat, I spun around searching for Ethan. I gasped. "Holy shit!" He was several feet away, his head barely visible above the water.

Tossed one direction, then another, like I'd been cast into a washing machine, I swam toward him, panicked, my heart racing. Losing sight of him again as another wave crashed into my face, I stopped to cough, only to breathe in more water. Wiping the water from my eyes, I saw him several feet away from me. Terrified and wide-eyed, Ethan whipped his head side to side as he tried in vain to keep the water from splashing directly into his face.

I finally reached him, and he climbed up on my shoulders, pushing me underwater. I surfaced and looked for shore as he climbed atop me again. "Oh, God," I said as I went under, taking in a big gulp of water. I surfaced again, coughing, and couldn't see over the waves. It was like we were in a liquid canyon.

The walls of water prevented me from getting Ethan on his back to find our way out of the turbulence. All I could do was hold him by the waist and push him toward the sky while I plunged down below the surface, intending to push off from the bottom. But there was no bottom.

I swam desperately toward the disk of light the bright summer sun formed at the water's surface, but we were still sinking. Then my arms and legs gave out, and a very peaceful feeling overtook me as I gazed down at Ethan, his arms extended gently at shoulder height and his beautiful halo of hair glistening in the rays of light penetrating the water all around us. Images of our ten years together, laughter and love amidst so much pain, flashed through my mind. Bonded in both life and death, feeling grateful to him for changing my life, my last thought was, *I won't be able to tell his story.*

2 Battlefield Promotion

A CYBORG BABY, THAT'S what Ethan looked like. Wires and tubes were connected to almost every part of his body. There was even an IV attached to the top of his head.

Ethan's breathing had sounded coarse after he was born shortly before midnight twelve hours before. When the nurses were not able to suction him effectively, they called in a ringer, a colleague known for her ability to get tubes down a throat where all others failed. Everyone was relieved when she seemed to get it down farther. Then, the tube suddenly popped up through his nose, producing raised eyebrows all around. They took him for X-rays.

Someone led Janet, her mom Aleta, and me to an adjoining room and suggested we get some sleep. Janet, after sixteen hours of labor and a sleeping pill, readily complied. Aleta lay down on a cot and perhaps slept. I was too busy fretting to notice. I sat in a reclining chair, stared at the ceiling, and anxiously reviewed a series of scenarios, each more unsettling than the previous one: 1. Misdiagnosis that takes all night to resolve, leaving us all exhausted but soon on our way back to a normal life; 2. Small defect in his esophagus that requires minor surgery, a limited hospital stay, and some unspecified follow-up care; 3. Severe defect in his esophagus that requires major surgery and

God only knows what else; 4. No esophagus, requiring he become part of some Marvel comic book–like secret government experiment to give him an artificial one; 5. An as yet unimaginable problem with an infinite range of potentially distressing consequences.

Only one thing was certain: this was more than I bargained for. When Janet was pregnant, she'd read everything she could get her hands on about pregnancy and child-rearing. While she gave me executive summaries of her findings, I silently wondered what all the fuss was about. *Why would she worry so much about something as ordinary as parenting?* I asked myself. *People have been doing it for centuries. Surely, it can't be that difficult.*

Once the baby was born, I expected life to return to normal, at least to what I understood as normal. I would busy myself with teaching, research, exercise, and travel as Janet and various professionals shepherded our child into happy adulthood. I might occasionally be charged with dropping the kid off at a babysitter, school, a playdate, or some activity. Most of my free time would be devoted to setting up social gatherings with an ever-widening circle of friends, whose kids, like ours, were extras in the ongoing drama that was life centered on me.

I clung to that vision of parenting at 3:00 a.m. when the lights came on and two young women entered the room. They introduced themselves as radiologists. One of them slapped an X-ray up onto a light box on the wall.

Janet and I gasped when the other said, "It is not even clear from the X-rays how much of an esophagus he has."

Janet began to cry. I stared at the wall, unable to move.

"Sir," one said, calling me to attention, "do you understand what I'm explaining to you?"

I responded, "Yes," though all I heard her say was that they would have to transfer him to Children's Memorial Hospital for a full diagnosis and possible treatment.

And that was merely the opening salvo. Janet was so exhausted from sixteen hours of labor, she remained at Prentice Women's Hospital for the rest of the day, while I went to Children's with Ethan. I was stunned. A voice deep inside me cried out in desperation. *What? You're putting me in charge?*

Janet was the family's responsible adult, not me. During our fourteen years of marriage, she had managed the mundane details of our lives together. Anything requiring patient attention like house closings, health insurance plans, retirement accounts? No worries. I relied on Janet to listen carefully and respond appropriately while I waited impatiently for her to show me where to sign. Extremely hyperactive, I handled everything that involved energetic movement: shopping, cooking, preparing for and managing parties, outings, and trips. Neither of us bothered much with cleaning.

Then, at age forty-two, without warning, training, or experience, I was suddenly given command. I had to sit still, pay attention, ask relevant questions, remember the answers, and perhaps even make momentous decisions. There was no recourse to my stock coping strategies, like slipping away unnoticed to exercise, read, go for a cup of coffee or a drink, hobnob with friends, or watch a movie. The spotlight was on me. The ball in my court. I was terrified.

I was so deep in thought about the unsettling turn of events that I jumped when someone touched my forearm. It was Janet's sister, Leslie. She and her three-year-old daughter, Lanika, had driven to Chicago from Michigan for Ethan's birth with Janet's parents, Rob and Aleta. Leslie, Rob, and Aleta had been rotating every two hours between staying with Janet at the maternity hospital, Lanika at the hotel, and me in the neonatal intensive care unit (NICU) since Ethan and I had arrived at Children's around 8:00 a.m., a little over four hours before. Leslie and I had stood silently at Ethan's crib for about half an hour before a young woman in a white lab coat, pushing a little cart with a desktop printer-sized device on it, walked up to us. She said she had to do an echocardiogram to check for heart defects, which were known to occur with Ethan's condition.

I shivered as she spread petroleum jelly over Ethan's chest and was relieved when she began moving an instrument that resembled a grocery store barcode reader across the gooey surface, thinking it might generate some heat. As she moved the instrument, images appeared on a monitor while a printout with squiggly lines streamed out the other end. The images displayed his heart and vascular systems from different angles, along with blood flow and heart movements. Each heartbeat produced rapid, multicolored explosions.

Now, this is fascinating, I thought, welcoming the distraction. While I watched this extraordinary home movie of Ethan's heart, he held my pinky finger with his free hand. I stroked the back of his neck with my other hand. Feeling helpless and jittery, I told him about an extraordinary footnote on the American concept of rights in Hegel's *Philosophy of Right.* It was all I could think of to talk about right then.

Twenty minutes later, I left for a quick bathroom break. I didn't get far before Leslie called out from behind me, "The doctor needs you to come back right away."

"Whatever you were doing before," the technician said, "do it again please. We can't continue the test when he's so agitated."

Ethan arched his back and waved his arms and legs wildly. His face was beet red as he tried to cry. He had the oddest silent cry that first day. Opening his mouth and tilting his head back like he was preparing to roar, he could produce only a very hoarse, hollow-sounding squeak. His lungs filled with stomach acid no doubt had a lot to do with it.

Resuming my monologue, I stroked his neck, and he wrapped his wee hand around my finger, suddenly becoming very calm. As he lay flat, his complexion returned to normal, and he stopped crying. Someone tapped my shoulder. A nurse needed something from under Ethan's crib. I moved around to the head of the bed and pressed myself flush against the metal railing to make room for another nurse with a med cart to pass, straining so that I would not pull my finger from his little hand.

The NICU was being remodeled, so it was cramped and noisy. In addition to the usual bell-and-whistle sounds of high-tech medical equipment, workmen busy behind thick plastic screens hammered and drilled. Earlier I had been aware of the buzz of activity around me, much like an animal in the wild, watchful for predators; now my attention was so completely focused on his little face that I was startled when the technician thanked me for calming him down. *Huh?* I glanced at her before returning my gaze to Ethan. *You mean I did that?* Conscious of all the purposeful movement throughout the room, it was like I was watching the scene through a soundproof glass enclosure; none of the commotion penetrated the little cocoon I shared with Ethan. Tears welled up in my eyes. By taking my finger in his itty-bitty hand, I felt like he was asking me to take care of him.

In a chance encounter the day before he was born, a new mother had asked us which musical compositions we had exposed Ethan to in utero. "Studies have shown that this does wonders for your baby's development," she said, arms akimbo, skeptical about our qualifications as new parents.

All we'd had to offer Ethan in his cozy fetal staging area was the endless chatter of two hopeless lip flappers. Apparently, it had paid off. He recognized my voice and took comfort in it. There were times in my life when I'd felt useful, helping others solve problems or contributing to a joint effort. But this was different. I could make a difference in his life, right then when he was so fragile and vulnerable. I was grateful that he chose me.

I was suddenly very calm, at peace with myself and with my surroundings, not buffeted by waves of nervous energy, disparate thoughts, or edginess as I always had been since a childhood bout with encephalitis. It was like a moment out of time. I stared at him in amazement, charmed by his little hand wrapped around my finger, marveling at the composed look on his tiny red face.

The moment passed, the feeling of calm swept away by all-too-familiar internal storms, electrical impulses firing uncontrollably, searching for an outlet. "You should reconsider, little guy," I mumbled. *Just glance at my HR file. Anxious, moody, short-tempered, hyperactive, self-involved; seeks limelight while shirking responsibility; performs well at social gatherings.* Ethan seemed unmoved. I shook my head. "Well, don't blame me later."

I shifted my weight from one foot to the other and back several times and scanned the crowded NICU, as though I expected it to be different than it had been only a few minutes before. Terrified that I wasn't up to the task of caring for him, I imagined it was a big mistake, that as doctors and nurses wheeled him to the operating room, someone would run up holding a folder aloft and gasp, "I'm so glad I caught you. We had the wrong X-ray. Your child is fine. Sorry for the inconvenience."

Before I could cue up another anxiety-relieving fantasy, a real transport team arrived to take Ethan away to perform a nonimaginary surgery on his esophagus and trachea. I looked down at Ethan, perhaps for the last time. "I won't disappoint you," I whispered, full of self-doubt.

As I watched them wheel Ethan away, Rob appeared at my side, and before I could ask him how Janet was doing, a nurse arrived to take us to a meeting with the surgeons. We were shown into a small office where two doctors sat at a desk, folders open at various angles. I had the odd feeling of being called into the principal's office, though neither of them had a disapproving air about them. They introduced themselves as Doctors Luck and Bambini.

Instead of a standard "Nice to meet you," I blurted out, "Lucky Baby. With names like that, we have nothing to worry about."

Rob smiled politely; the doctors were unmoved.

I guess they've heard that one before.

"Ethan has a condition known as tracheoesophageal fistula. TEF for short," Dr. Luck, the lead surgeon, said in a calm, measured tone. "In other words, his esophagus ends in a pouch at the top of his throat. It is not clear from the X-rays," she continued, "how much of an esophagus he has."

I struggled to stay with her explanation. It was all very clearly stated. Nothing was difficult to grasp intellectually. But I was stuck on the phrase "how much of an esophagus he has." It felt like I was in the event horizon of a black hole, where the gravity stopped everything and even time came to a standstill. Some very small, unaffected portion of my brain noticed Dr. Luck still spoke directly to me, not Rob. Her gaze dislodged my mind from its orbit around that phrase. I rejoined her explanation.

"Once we operate, we can determine precisely the condition of his esophagus," she continued. "For now, the goal is to close it off from the trachea and ensure stomach acid is not seeping into the trachea and then down into his lungs."

Whoa, another black hole. I struggled to focus my eyes on her gaze in order to break orbit again. Pushing, pushing, I broke free and caught up.

"Once this surgery is completed," she said, "we will confer with other specialists, such as the cardiologists, about his other problems, and how they can best be treated." She put some papers in a folder, then asked, "Do you have any other questions?"

I was relieved when Rob picked up on the cue and asked a few. He was an unusually calm and focused person. With his perfect recall and careful notetaking, I was confident I could query him later about his questions and her responses. This freed me to shift my mind back to those troubling phrases.

Dr. Luck excused herself. Dr. Bambini, a surgical fellow probably in his mid-thirties, looked at me with soft brown eyes and said, "Ethan's problems are on the benign side of serious." *He's clearly the good cop.* "Without treatment," he continued, "they are life-threatening conditions. But they are correctible. It will take some time and an indeterminate amount of remedial care. But they are correctible."

Oh, I liked that word—*cor-rect-ible.* That would be my mantra, I resolved, repeating it several times as I breathed deeply whenever I was in danger of being stuck at a medical explanation event horizon.

Dr. Bambini said we had a couple of hours before Ethan would be ready for surgery. Rob went to the maternity hospital to update Janet while I hurried to the stairs like someone escaping a burning building. Loping along Fullerton Avenue toward Lake Michigan, I thought about the moment with Ethan in the NICU, the unfamiliar feeling of calm I had when he wrapped his little hand around my finger. I had never experienced anything like that before. Encephalitis at age four had left me extremely hyperactive, anxious, jittery, quick to anger, and subject to wild mood swings. These were my constant companions. Ethan's touch kept them at bay, if only briefly. *How?* I had no idea. It seemed magical.

When I reached the busy intersection at Clark Street, someone pushed past me, turning me sideways to face a shop window. In the reflection, I noticed the bloodstains on my white pants, clearly a poor fashion choice for labor and delivery. Waiting for the traffic light, I saw a clothing store on the other side of the intersection. And with a coffee shop right next door. *Perfect.*

Thumbing through piles of dark-colored trousers, images of the violence of the birth flashed through my mind. No one had warned me it would be so bloody. Maybe that was covered in one of Janet's in-services I had tuned out, along with what *not* to wear to the hospital for the birth of your child. The carnage required to get the little guy out of her had sent me into a temporary state of shock. I had stood wide-eyed as the doctor stitched her up afterward and was only drawn out of my trance when I felt Janet's hand in mine.

"Thank you for the root beer, my love. It was a nice surprise." She smiled, and her eyes sparkled despite the trial she had endured. Her unfailing good cheer was one of the many things I loved about her.

"Sure," I responded, having forgotten the doctor suggested I bring something along for her. It was only happenstance that I had it with me. I had bought it a couple days before and absentmindedly left it in my bag.

Now, I decided on a pair of black slacks and a long-sleeve purple turtleneck shirt to wear in the chilly hospital, along with several additional pairs of pants and shirts. Newly outfitted, I carried two overstuffed shopping bags and a reassuringly large cup of coffee down Fullerton Avenue to the hospital.

When I reached the NICU, the nurse said they had prepped Ethan for surgery more quickly than they anticipated. I dashed off to the elevator and got off at the second floor. Running down the hall, I noticed a surgical team wheeling toward me from an adjoining hallway. I tried to stop, but the momentum produced by the bulk and weight of my shopping bags caused me to skid a few feet across the floor.

They stopped and introduced themselves. I dropped my bags and fought back tears while trying to think of something to say. We shared a moment of companionable silence. Finally, I leaned down and said, "I love you, Ethan." I blew him a kiss and added, "Please don't leave me now." I smiled at the surgical team arrayed on the other side of the gurney, then said, "Whatever happens, I know that you did all you could to save him. We will always be very grateful."

Several of them nodded before they all hurried down the hall and through two automatic doors. I stood there for so long that people started to make their way around me like I was a human traffic circle. I moved with my bags over to one side of the hallway, leaned against the wall, and cried as I thought about the possibility of Ethan not surviving the surgery. He had wrapped his little fingers around my heart. *How can I bear to lose him now?*

The doors opened again. It was one of the nurses from the NICU, who escorted me to the empty surgical waiting room. She said there were no other surgeries scheduled, so I would have the place to myself. Not surprising, as it was Labor Day evening. I sat in a rather uncomfortable chair and began paging through a *People* magazine. An article about what the stars of popular sitcoms from the '80s and '90s were doing at the dawn of the new millennium caught my attention. I shook my head as I paged through the photos. I hadn't watched any of the shows while they were on the air, and the stars were barely recognizable to me despite their apparent fame.

"This is what Janet must have meant when she said I should bring some light reading," I whispered. Painfully aware that bringing Joseph Conrad's *Heart of Darkness* might have been a mistake, I rooted around in a huge pile of magazines for something else to read. *I'd kill for a* National Enquirer *right now.*

The television was on in the corner of the room with the sound barely audible. Otherwise, the room was eerily quiet. I called Janet. She'd been sleeping and was still groggy. After discussing Ethan's condition and how she was feeling, I confessed I wasn't sure I had the right skill set for this new line of work.

"I think you'll do fine. You're good in a crisis. It's one of the things I love most about you."

"I thought it was my cool glasses and party-planning skills."

"Well, those too," she responded. "I'll admit, you can be a bit of a handful at times. Your little brother Chris was right about that. But you also always seem to rise to the occasion. Remember when we were camping and all our wood got wet? You were so desperate to make coffee that you managed to get a fire going. If you want something bad enough, you can do it. Do you want to help him get through this?"

"Yes, yes, I do," I said.

"Then you'll find a way."

After I hung up, I started to move toward the TV when Rob and Aleta came through the door with some sandwiches and an iced mocha chaser for me. *What a relief!* I was starving, and it was great to have some company.

Several hours passed. The air-conditioning roared. The level must have been set earlier in the day when the room was packed with anxious people radiating heat. With the room empty except for us, it felt like a meat locker.

A little sleepy, we turned off the TV and found some clean sheets piled on a chair by the door. Rob lay across a couch with his head turned toward the back. Wound up in a sheet, he looked like a giant

Wiener Wrap. Aleta opted for an upright chair, her feet resting atop an end table, with the sheet pulled up to her nose. I stood watch, staring blankly out a window.

Dr. Luck appeared at the entryway around 10:00 p.m. Anticipating another attention deficit incident, I woke Rob. Dr. Luck stood with her arms folded, matching Rob in terms of the calm she exuded. I, by contrast, vibrated with nervous energy, a combination of being cooped up inside most of the day and anxiety over Ethan's condition.

"The surgery went fine," she said. "He has a fully formed esophagus, which is good. We don't know the condition of the esophagus and how well it will work. But we were able to attach it in its proper position. There is a serious narrowing of his aorta, along with some other heart defects. Some of these will have to be corrected surgically. The cardiologists and cardiovascular surgeons will talk with you about that tomorrow. He is in postoperative recovery right now and should be transferred to the NICU very soon."

We silently filed out of the hospital. After walking Rob and Aleta to their car, I stood at the five-way crossing on Lincoln Avenue south of the hospital and watched people hurry past me in every direction. I was dazed by all the activity, as though I had emerged from some artificially induced hibernation. A gentle breeze caressed my back, and my limbs began to move. I found myself walking down Lincoln Avenue. On either side of the street, bars were filled with people. For early September, it was still quite warm. Giant windows opened wide with groups of people huddled around small round tables, laughing and talking. Fast-food restaurants had delivery cars double-parked. People got into and out of cabs, stumbling a bit from side to side. It felt odd that I didn't want to stop in for a drink. I imagined they were part of a partying humans exhibit in a futuristic zoo and I was on the lam from the terrified parents' section.

Threading my way around a large intersection packed with cars and people, I was drawn to a triangular brick building with a passageway slicing through the middle of it. Tucked in the little passageway was a set of stairs, which led down to a pizza place. I made a mental note to go back there at some point with Janet and Ethan, having momentarily forgotten Ethan faced an uncertain future.

Soon, I stood across the street from the hospital again. My heart raced as I thought about how miscast I was in this role. By taking my finger in his little hand, however, Ethan had made it clear that he expected the performance of a lifetime.

People hurried past, some in surgical scrubs. My stint as officer of the day was not over. I crossed the street and followed some nurses up the stairs to the emergency room entrance. Walking back into the hospital, I shook my head and headed for the NICU. *Adulthood, ready or not, here I come.*

3 Crisis du Jour

"WHAT'S THE PROBLEM, MA'AM?" the firefighter asked, an axe slung over his shoulder.

"I gave my baby too much blood pressure medication," Janet whispered. Nestled in Janet's arms, Ethan extended a hand toward the rim of the man's helmet, then smiled at Janet.

"Blood pressure medication?" A second firefighter's face was illuminated by flashing lights in the street.

The murmured phrase, "blood pressure medication," circulated among the neighbors gathered on the sidewalk. The firefighters left with an air of disappointment, as did the neighbors, except for the block's oldest residents, both puffing cigarettes, and a young mom wearing an oversized Bears jersey.

Janet and I talked with the EMT about how to get Ethan to the hospital. The problem was the ambulance didn't have a seat appropriate for a three-month-old baby. The neighborhood delegation was arrayed behind us like a Greek chorus. They frowned and shook their heads in unison as we discussed options. The hair on the back of my neck rose as I sensed a lecture coming. It wouldn't have been the first. It seemed as if every time we poked our heads out of the house, someone was there to give us unsolicited advice.

Earlier that day, I was standing in our front room when our next-door neighbor called through the side window, "Jeff, what do you intend to do about those newspapers?"

We had been so busy reinserting feeding tubes down Ethan's nose, tending to his barky cough from aspirating breast milk, and fretting about his surgically repaired aorta that we'd neglected to bring in our newspapers for several days.

We were the first to admit we were unprepared to be parents and blurted out in unison when Janet's water broke, "What were we thinking?" But as Janet's mom—mother of five—put it, there were no standard operating procedures for a baby with Ethan's palette of health challenges. We were walking in the dark, afraid of tripping at each step. As I saw it, our self-appointed life coaches weren't showing the way out of the darkness so much as reminding us how lost we were.

"How about we jerry-rig our own infant seat?" Janet asked when the young mom, a pediatric nurse, took a step forward to serve as the evening's chorus leader.

I was already miffed about the trip to Children's Memorial. Cooped up inside all day, I was desperate to get out of the house, but not if it was for yet another trip to the doctor or the hospital. Besides, this was the one part of the day I had come to enjoy, the midnight tube feedings. Sitting in a reclining chair, covered in blankets, Ethan on my chest, breathing softly, was the only chance I got to do any reading. Right then I was completely engrossed in Livy's *The War with Hannibal*. Reading about crossing the Alps atop elephants sure beat sitting in a hospital waiting room.

Now, before spending hours, or perhaps days, in the hospital, we had to have a performance review? I felt Janet's hand on my forearm. She sensed an outburst in the making and wanted to head it off. Her apprehension was understandable. I struggled to control my temper even under the best of conditions. The constant supervision, questioning, probing, and advising, while perhaps well-intentioned, kept me at a near boil much of the time. Two days before, I had blown up at the de facto head of the block's parenting quality control board. She had stopped us on our way to an appointment with Ethan's ENT specialist. Janet explained to her how Ethan's swallowing challenges might be due to mouth sensitivity produced by the ten days he had spent on a ventilator as a newborn.

"Oh, brother," she responded with a dismissive wave. "Don't be so fussy. Just jam the bottle into his mouth until he starts sucking."

"You have no idea what you're talking about!" I yelled. Janet had placed her hand on my forearm then too. I added a parting shot anyway. "And mind your own fucking business!" She stormed off in a huff.

Anger again welled up inside me when the Bears fan said, "No, no, no! Hold on a minute here." After a sigh, she continued, "Why don't you let me have a look at him? I might save you a trip to the hospital."

Wait, what? Finally, a useful suggestion. "Great idea!" I said.

The chorus nodded with approval, while Janet stared at me with a blank expression. For her that was the equivalent of an angry glare.

"Thank you so much," Janet responded. "That is a very kind offer. But we've already called the cardiac staff at Children's. They said we should get there as soon as we can."

The chorus disbanded. Clouds of smoke moved in opposite directions as they made their way into houses on either side of us, while the EMTs and I walked to the ambulance to position the car seat.

With Ethan securely fastened and Janet and me sitting uncomfortably in the back of the ambulance, the paramedics dropped another bomb. They were required by law to take us to the nearest medical facility, which was the Edgewater Medical Center a few blocks away, not Children's Hospital.

The ER waiting area was packed. Janet took the last available chair and held Ethan, who slept peacefully, while I leaned up against a column next to them and thought about the mishap with the medication. It was only one of the many meds Ethan received several times a day through the feeding tube in his nose. We filled the syringes one after another and set them up in a row before sending them into the tube. The blood pressure medication stood out from the others because it was such a tiny amount. Under the best of conditions, it was difficult to not overfill the syringe, and this day had involved less-than-ideal conditions.

Janet had spent the entire day caring for Ethan. She met with therapists, telephoned doctors, expressed breast milk, and did complex calculations of how much milk to give him through the feeding tube. Exhausted, she had accidentally switched the blood pressure medication dosage with the one for reflux, which was much larger.

More people filed into the already crowded waiting room and positioned themselves along the wall opposite me. It was hard to believe that barely a year before we were living in London, where our biggest worry then was deciding how to celebrate the new millennium. To get my mind off the state of things, I asked Janet, "Can you believe that both Hillary Clinton and John Wayne Gacy were born in this hospital?"

"We're in fine company indeed," Janet said. "You know, I've been thinking about Ethan's blood pressure medication. It was my fault tonight, I get that. It was careless of me. But I still wonder about the dosage. Everything I've read suggests we should be giving him more."

"Such a wee bit," I said. "It's almost the medication equivalent of an extra-extra-dry martini; you wave the bottle over the syringe without actually putting anything in it."

She smiled. We shared a quiet moment before rescue workers charged into the room with a man on a gurney writhing in pain. A bloody sheet covered his abdomen. "A gunshot victim, no doubt," a man whispered into my ear. Startled, I reared back my head and nodded at his toothless smile. The smell of alcohol on his breath made me long for a drink myself. He stumbled back across the room, and my attention returned to the EMTs, who disappeared into an exam room on the far side of the waiting area. We could still hear the muffled sound of screams after they closed the door.

"Welcome to the neighborhood," I said to Janet, who nodded with raised eyebrows. "You know, mob movies teach that gunshot wounds to the abdomen are the most painful."

The screaming grew louder briefly as the medics left the exam room and closed the door behind them. Walking past us, they caught sight of Ethan and stopped to chat. One asked to hold him and seemed rather put out when Janet politely declined. Over the next hour, a number of other people from the waiting room made the same request and appeared equally annoyed when we said no. Our explanation that Ethan was on a modified quarantine didn't satisfy them.

They might have thought differently had they heard Dr. Luck's stern warning about contagions. In Ethan's weakened state, a so-called common cold might land him in the hospital for an extended stay. Something like the respiratory syncytial virus (RSV) could be life-threatening. Consequently, we had to limit his contact with people as much as possible. Anyone holding him should wear a gown and rubber gloves, even a face mask if they were sick.

Even with that fresh in our memory, it was still hard for Janet. She wanted to share her baby with the world. But what made it especially difficult was her powerful instinct to try to make people happy.

Denying others what they wanted, even strangers, was emotionally draining for her.

Someone with a large lump on his forehead ambled up to Janet and Ethan when a nurse called our name and led us to a curtained bed in the corner. After a few minutes, a young physician joined us and began the examination. He listened to Ethan's heart and lungs, checked his throat, felt his abdomen, and even examined his ears. "He seems fine," the doctor said. "But to be safe, I think you should take him to Children's. They are better positioned to treat any complications from the excessive medication."

"You have got to be kidding," I said to Janet, burning with anger, after the doctor left the room. "*Now* on to Children's?"

"Calm down," Janet said. "It will be fine."

"Define *fine*."

After fastening the car seat safely into yet another ambulance, we made our way to Children's, arriving three hours after I'd first called poison control. I shook my head, remembering the feeling of urgency then.

"How fast can you get to Children's?" they had asked.

Twenty minutes. No, wait. Three hours.

Now, we sat in the ER waiting room and watched fish flitter in a huge aquarium. My mind drifted back to the harrowing first hours after Ethan was born, when we were still at Prentice Women's Hospital waiting for Ethan to be transferred to Children's for emergency surgery.

The transport team had arrived with a portable incubator. Full of wires and monitoring screens, it looked more like a personal spaceship than a crib. It was hard to believe that such a contraption was necessary to convey a newborn baby—a good-sized overcoat pocket would have been sufficient. When the attendants approached Janet to take Ethan, she turned away and tightened her grip around him. Everyone had turned to me to do something.

I took a deep breath and knelt down by the front corner of the wheelchair. I slowly adjusted the blanket across her legs and tucked it up around her arms while I tried to think of something to say.

"Are you warm enough?"

She nodded. She stroked his tiny head with her index finger and sang a lullaby while tears ran down her cheeks. I put my arm around her and placed the top of my head against hers. We talked a bit about how cute he was. She gave him a few kisses and looked up at me with tired eyes.

"You know," I said, "forty years ago, Children's Memorial Hospital saved my life. I know they'll save his as well."

"Okay," she whispered, gently relinquishing him to the ambulance driver, who whisked him away with great efficiency.

My mom had told me that many times while I was growing up, since I had been so sick. *Who knew whether it was true or not?* I was just glad it popped into my head. During our fourteen years of marriage, I had a tendency of saying the wrong thing at important moments. I was relieved to have gotten it right for once.

Now at Children's again, a fish, barely visible except for its eyes on the sides of its wafer-thin face, gazed at me. It rotated slowly and swam off. I scanned the waiting room and felt very much at home.

"It's good we are here," I said to Janet, who nodded without turning toward me. "And I'm sorry that I was a little cranky earlier. I guess it wasn't helping."

"No, it was not," she said.

A cardiology resident called our name and then led us into an exam room. She was about six months pregnant. When she pressed close to Ethan to listen to his chest with a stethoscope, he reached out and put his tiny hands on her tummy and gave her a big smile. She smiled at him and rubbed his head affectionately. While reading his file, she asked about his dosage and seemed surprised by our response. She scribbled some numbers on her pad and completed several calculations before leaving to confer with the attending physician.

"There appears to be a misunderstanding," she said upon her return a few minutes later. "By my calculations, you've been giving him too little blood pressure medication."

"How much should we be giving him?" Janet asked.

"Well, interestingly, about three times what you gave him tonight."

There was a stunned silence as we took this in, and we laughed. Having misread the discharge instructions from the NICU, we had been seriously under medicating him all along.

"I guess he's not going to be having a heart attack," I said.

"I think not," the doctor responded. "In fact, you can stop giving him this medication, since he is obviously doing great without it."

In no time, we were speeding up Lake Shore Drive in a cab. Looking out at the lake, I said, "Next time, we should have the neighbors check him out first."

Janet didn't respond. I glanced over to find her fast asleep and Ethan smiling at me. I kissed him and he shook his arms excitedly, prompting me to smile and forget for a moment that I was in way over my head.

4 The Tower of Babble

AT 6:00 A.M., I rushed up the back stairs of Children's Hospital, a breakfast sandwich and newspaper pressed under my left elbow and a cup of joe gripped tightly in my right hand. Hot coffee spilled out from under the lid, causing me to wince, but I didn't slow down. There wasn't a second to spare. Janet had stayed overnight and needed to leave by 7:00 a.m. for an early meeting. Having postponed indefinitely my search for a teaching job, I was available to spend the day in the hospital.

Ethan had had a grisly surgery the day before to implant a feeding tube into his stomach, which required Dr. Luck to tear a hole directly through his abdominal wall. Poor little feller. Lips quivering, his head turning side to side, he was clearly in a lot of pain. It reminded me of the guy we'd seen a month before at the Edgewater Medical Center with the gunshot wound to the stomach. The EMTs could hardly keep him on the gurney because the pain caused him to shake so violently. At four and a half months old, Ethan was not in danger of falling out of his crib. Still, it was agonizing to watch him cry softly all day, powerless to help him.

Thinking he might need rest, we sat silently the entire day. We might as well have had a dance party with strobe lights and pulsating music because Ethan's roommate, a young boy around seven or eight years old, had an endless stream of visitors who watched TV on high volume and engaged in high-decibel phone conversations. When they weren't yelling at the TV or shouting on the phone, they argued bitterly with one another about sports or the stock market. Not to be overlooked, the patient often interrupted, barking out complaints—"hot," "cold," "thirsty," "tired"—and orders—"turn channel," "get juice," "move pillow."

After a long day of endless racket, the neighbor's guests left, the TV went silent, and there were no more phone calls. Janet and I looked at each other a little surprised by the sudden quiet. Ethan, perhaps startled by the silence, woke up and began to cry. The mother of the boy in the next bed poked her head around the curtain and glared at us to let us know it was the Dauphin's bedtime. I left the hospital itching for a fight.

The next morning, I couldn't stop thinking about the roommate and his thoughtless support team as I charged up the stairs. As I made the final turn, the door to the fifth floor in view, my heart raced. Images of us shaking our fists at one another with our faces contorted in anger flashed through my mind. Suddenly, Janet's sad countenance appeared in the fight scene montage. *How'd that get there?* Striding down the hall, concerned that I might say something Janet would regret, I thought to myself, *Just look left. Don't make eye contact.* When I entered the room, I was surprised to find Janet and the nurse talking quietly near an empty bed. "You have to understand what they're going through," the nurse said.

Janet nodded with a concerned smile. After the nurse left, Janet peeked around the curtain at Ethan, then explained, "The neighbor had complained about Ethan moaning. The nurse didn't want us to take it personally. She said they were under a lot of strain."

"Who isn't?" I responded.

Not offering me a chance to elaborate, Janet continued, "Last night, though, the mom and I finally had a laugh. Her son woke up and began calling out for her, which woke Ethan up. Then he began to cry. The tables were turned. She laughed, which broke the tension."

"There was plenty of that to go around," I said, feeling frazzled.

After Janet left for work, I brooded about the possibility a phase shift might occur amidst all this tension. As a kid, after encephalitis, my brain wave patterns often suddenly went haywire, which caused seizures and a complete change in demeanor. In a flash, I went from calm and gentle to agitated and even wild. It still happened, though less frequently and with less dramatic effects. Janet said it was like I became another person. My eyes squinted as though my brain swelled and pressed against my skull. I didn't know what caused these symptoms, only that they tended to occur at times of great stress. I believe my brain adapted after encephalitis, rewiring itself in some ways, and yet still could become overtaxed in trying times.

Whatever the cause, these episodes were quite unsettling. They felt like an out-of-body experience, though not in some comfy, mystical sort of way. Disconnected from my own mind and body, on the outside looking in with no control over myself, I lost track of what I did and was unable to process what people said to me. My body became a placeholder until everything snapped back into alignment. Fortunately, no one was ever harmed. Most people, as far as I could tell, didn't even notice. *What if one occurred while I was taking care of Ethan?* Merely picking him up out of his crib was a feat while he was connected to all those wires and tubes. *How about when central command goes off-line?*

Ethan was awake. The nurse helped us settle into the reclining chair, where we read for a while. It was the first time I'd held him in a chair since the surgery. I expected it would be too painful for him, with the angry red skin pressing more firmly against the hard plastic tubing. But he didn't cry or flinch the entire time. Snuggling with him made me feel better too.

With Ethan back in his crib, sleeping fitfully, my gaze shifted to the weak winter sun shining through the window. I longed to get outside, walk around, get some exercise, and maybe read at a coffee shop. Glancing at my watch, I blurted out, "Only nine thirty!"

What Dr. Seuss called the "waiting place" was a living hell for a hyperactive person like me. In grade school, I often put my ear against telephone poles in the alley to feel the powerful vibrations of the electrical currents coursing through the lines. That's how I felt all the time. It was like lightning bolts striking inside me constantly.

A nurse arrived, checked Ethan's dressing, and serviced the feeding tube apparatus. It was an elaborate process, which she executed effortlessly.

"Operating this thing is a little scary at first for everyone," she said. "You will get the hang of it."

"Thanks. I hope so. Right now, it feels like we are defusing a bomb. Each step takes forever, and we breathe a sigh of relief before we begin the next one."

"You can get a job with the bomb squad after this is all over," she said with a reassuring tap on my shoulder.

I dozed off and woke to find Dr. Luck and a group of medical students and residents surrounding Ethan's crib. I surveyed the array of colorful scrubs and lab coats. The hospital culture had a medieval quality to it—the color of the uniform indicated each person's position within the medical staff hierarchy. I looked down at my shirt, light blue with a chocolate stain. *Where do I belong in the facility's feudal order?*

Dr. Luck interrupted my musings to ask me how Ethan was doing. *What a loaded question!* Willing to say anything to get him discharged, I considered responding, "He's fine." Knowing that wouldn't work, I settled for the truth, hoping it would be enough to spring him . . . and me. "He was in a lot of pain yesterday, but he seems much more comfortable today."

Then, the dreaded follow-up question. "Have you noticed any leaking where the tube enters his stomach?"

This put me on my guard. I felt like I was a suspect in a cop show where she knew the answer and was testing me. Ethan watched me. This definitely raised the stakes. *Will he possibly remember this as the first lie he heard me tell?*

To top it all off, I imagined Ethan nodding as Janet softly said, "You're a parent now, so you need to model good behavior."

I took a deep breath and told the truth. "Some."

Turning to the assembled crowd, Dr. Luck explained that a swallow study was done after we reported that Ethan was coughing while he nursed or took milk from a bottle. It showed he was aspirating, so a G-tube was inserted into his stomach. During the surgery, Dr. Holinger had conducted a thorough exam of his throat and airways and found a cleft in Ethan's larynx. The cleft was small enough that Dr. Holinger didn't need to insert a breathing tube into his throat. However, because the larynx never fully closed, Ethan would always tend to aspirate while swallowing, putting him at a greater risk of respiratory infections. The hope was that he would eventually learn to compensate for the defect and no longer need the G-tube.

Dr. Luck and her retinue left. I was overcome with sadness as I imagined Ethan with a tracheostomy tube in his little throat. I recalled how uncomfortable trach tubes were for the patients at the nursing home where I'd worked as an orderly twenty years before.

Nurses constantly swabbed the secretions that oozed out of them. But most of those people got traches late in life; our little guy was not yet five months old. *What will life be like for him? Will he be able to eat on his own or speak?*

Ethan smiled, and I felt reassured. I placed my pinky finger onto his palm, and he giggled as he wrapped his little hand around it like he'd done on his first day. Then he suddenly got a serious look on his face and moved his mouth to make a very soft sound. I bent down and turned my head sideways, hoping he would say it again. He reached up and grabbed my head with both hands and said, "Ba." We smiled at each other, and he continued, "Ba, ba, ba." He repeated this over and over, pausing to smile each time before he continued.

"I'm glad you're enjoying yourself," I said. "Any suggestions for what I can do?"

"Ba, ba, ba," he responded.

"Thanks. You're very helpful."

I sat down and wrote in my notebook, enjoying Ethan's babbling as background music. How ironic it was that he began babbling right after Dr. Luck discussed his laryngeal cleft, since the larynx contained his vocal cords. It also opened and closed while swallowing, which enabled one to breathe through the mouth as well as the nose—something someone might take for granted if he or she didn't have bad sinuses like me.

As remarkable as the larynx was, though, I wished I didn't know so much about it. I had learned to focus my mind on the most positive take on everything, in order to control my anxiety. Now, I instinctively screened out anything that might unsettle me. But there it was. I wasn't able to shield myself from the potential worries that Ethan's defective larynx caused. The fact that I could spell larynx correctly three out of four times indicated how serious the situation was. Alas, the potential problems this little gap created could not simply be willed away.

The food cart arrived at 10:45 a.m. I stocked up: several salads, both green and fruit varieties; a couple of sandwiches; small bags of chips and pretzels; rice cakes, crackers, and sugary bottled coffee drinks; several cans of fizzy water; chocolate bars; and some gum. Flustered, the guy glanced over my shoulder as I rattled off my order. He must have wondered how many people were in the room with me. I carried everything inside and organized it all on the floor next to the wall. My intention was it would last the entire day and help me pass the time. The tentative schedule would be a sandwich with water and chips around 11:30; the fruit salad and a coffee drink around 1:00; pretzels, rice cakes, and a coffee drink around 3:00; a sandwich, water, coffee drink, and chocolate around 5:00. I would have the green salad after Janet arrived. Everything was snarfed down by 1:30, leaving me bereft.

Time moved agonizingly slow for me the rest of the day. Ethan happily babbled away in his bed when he wasn't napping, listening to a story, or being tended to by the medical staff.

Janet returned from work around 6:00 p.m. to find me pacing back and forth by the window like a big cat at the zoo. I left the hospital shortly after 9:00 p.m. and returned early the next morning in despair about another day in the hospital. I froze after rounding the corner by the nurses' station. Several people gathered outside Ethan's room, some in street clothes and others in hospital garb. *Oh, no! He must have a new roommate.* "Please, Lord, let it be someone nice. Please, please, please," I whispered, to make sure no one heard me.

As I walked toward them, they nodded their heads and talked with big smiles, which put me at ease. From halfway down the hall, I heard Ethan babbling.

Everyone smiled at me when I joined the group. "It's so beautiful," a young woman in sweatpants said.

"It's like an operatic aria," someone in a white lab coat added.

I nodded, and we all listened to Ethan for a moment before they went on their way. I walked into the room and flinched when I saw Janet speaking with a nurse. *What now? Complaints about the babbling?*

I was relieved to learn it was a discharge nurse. I left Janet with her breakfast and went off for coffee, positively giddy about going home. After I went through the door to the back stairs, I stopped. It suddenly dawned on me that I would soon be completely on my own without the nursing staff to manage everything.

Maybe the hospital was not so bad after all.

5 Who Needs Ted?

EARLY ON A COLD February morning, a month after Ethan's G-tube surgery, I stirred my coffee while the café's owner, Ted, told me about the plumbing problems that had caused him to close for a few days. Ethan and I had spent a lot of time in his café, reading books and chatting with the regulars. It was kind of a community center for us. I was relieved he had reopened that morning.

"Hope to see Ethan with you again soon," Ted said as I turned to leave.

"Later today if I have anything to say about it."

I pushed the heavy door open with my shoulder and stepped out into a school of hurried commuters. I sipped my coffee while they weaved their way around me, then quickly crossed the street and entered the pharmacy.

"Back again so soon?" the pharmacist said. "That boy needs a lot of medication. How is he?"

"He's great, thanks," I said over my shoulder as I hustled out. As always, crackling with nervous energy, I was anxious to get a walk in before having to return home. I had learned my lesson the day before—twelve hours of unrelenting baby care without stepping a foot outside. I adjusted my scarf against the strong breeze, thinking longingly of a baby care version of the famous Marxist formula. Instead of working a lathe in the morning, fishing in the afternoon, and doing literary criticism at night, one does baby care in the morning, exercises and reads in the afternoon, and socializes at night.

I rounded the corner by the library and stopped at the alley for a standing car. It merged into traffic, and it was like a curtain in a play had been raised, revealing a different winter scene. Most of the sidewalks I had traversed that morning had been well shoveled. The long block before me had not been cleared and appeared to be completely trampled. Small, hard-packed mounds of snow caused my ankles to buckle; deep ruts with hardened edges often caught and held the ball of my foot. Fearing a sprained ankle or perhaps a fall, I reversed course and went to the next block up.

Even on the smooth pavement, my feet twisted and turned with each step, particularly my right foot, which was weaker and more deformed than its companion. The symptoms of the degenerative condition I inherited from my mom, Charcot-Marie-Tooth disease (CMT), were comparatively mild, according to a long list of experts. The pain in my feet suggested otherwise and reminded me of how much I missed my exercise talisman—lap swimming—because it reduced the high-voltage electric current, which coursed through me without taxing my legs.

I hadn't been near a pool since Ethan was born. There wasn't enough time in the day. We spent every spare minute caring for him, and the complexity of his treatments and risk of infection kept us from hiring babysitters. Stretching helped counteract the effects of the disease by forcing bones, tendons, and muscles into their proper position. But it had been hard to find time even for that recently. My feet would get worse and worse.

At the corner of our block, a black Lab added some color to the feet of a snowman some neighborhood kids and I had built.

"Hey!" I yelled to the owner, hurrying toward him. "Can't you find a tree or something?"

"Oh, sorry," he said, wide-eyed, before yanking on the dog's collar, too late to prevent our canine visitor from leaving a yellow trail across the snowman's feet.

Farther down the block, a neighbor tried to pull her car out of the deep snow. I pushed from behind as she rocked back and forth, spraying sludge-covered snow all over my pants and boots. Suddenly, the vehicle jumped the rut, then lurched backward, knocking me back into a parked car before it sped forward and careened into the street at an angle.

"Thanks a million," she said through the open passenger window. "I'm sorry to hear that Janet has gone back to work. We could all use more time with our kids."

"Indeed we could," I responded, waving as she drove down the street.

Walking toward our house, I recalled Uncle Maury asking me after I got my first teaching job if it bothered me that Janet made more money than I did. "Not nearly as badly than if she made less," I countered.

That was 1995, five years before we had Ethan. There wasn't much at stake then. Janet liked her job, and our income was fine. It mattered a lot more now. Janet, who gave every moment she could to Ethan and loved every second of it, would have preferred to work less or not at all while Ethan was young. But I couldn't make enough as a college professor to allow her not to work. The last teaching position I had before we moved to England in 1998 paid about a third of her current salary, and it was only a one-year position. Ethan was born shortly after we returned to the States in July of 2000. Even if I found a full-time position, Janet would still have to work at least part-time or probably even full-time next fall. So we were stuck in this difficult position, with her having too much career and me having too little.

Janet wasn't even an ambitious person. She really enjoyed being a librarian, but she didn't have great career aspirations. Being very conscientious and responsible, however, she always wanted to do a good job, which didn't go unnoticed. While in library school, she served as an intern at a global law firm. Then after graduation she stayed on as a research librarian and was gradually promoted into higher-level administrative positions, eventually leaving the library altogether. Now, she managed not one but two major departments. Hence the long hours, which left her drained, physically and emotionally. Yet she somehow found it in herself to shower both Ethan and me with love. She was truly a remarkable person, much better than I was certainly.

As I trudged slowly up our front steps, I saw Janet inside gathering up her things to go to work. "The countdown begins," I said under my breath.

"Good luck today," she said as she zipped up her backpack. "I hope you guys will be okay."

"Like Ozzie and Harriet."

I sighed and watched her drive down the alley before reading Ethan's care regimen for the day. I noticed there was a small gap between his physical therapy appointment and his noon feeding. *Get the therapist out the door a few minutes early, and off to the coffee shop.* "Yeah right," I said to my archnemesis, the care sheet, which for days had been the equivalent of a guard at the door keeping us under house arrest.

Ethan was watching his mobile and giggling when I walked into his room. When he saw me, he broke into a big smile. His eyes lit up, and he squirmed with delight. I picked him up and held him. We twirled around a bit with him smiling broadly, his arms extended like a kid thrilled to be on a roller coaster.

After changing his diaper, I checked his feeding tube. With a stethoscope pressed to his tummy, I pumped air into the tube until I heard it in his stomach. Ethan grabbed the round sensor piece, extended his arm to the side, and gazed at the device intently while he worked his little fingers around the entire unit. When he returned his attention to me, I said, "We are going to Ted's after physical therapy, little guy. What do you think?" He smiled and kicked his feet. *That kid was game for anything.*

I picked him up, swung him around a few times, and put him down in a bouncy chair. He watched me closely while I loaded the bag, primed the pump, and looked for kinks in the line. I wondered at what point his fine motor skills would be good enough to set up the tube feedings for himself.

Settled in the chair, the two of us enveloped by a comforter, I turned on the pump and began reading to him. He watched the wheel turn that pushed milk through the line, then his eyes followed the milk moving slowly down the tube before he returned his attention to me. After I read him a few stories, he closed his eyes and fell asleep. Pushing the chair back into a slightly reclined position, I flipped him over onto my chest and listened to the rhythmic clicking of the wheel. The sun shone brightly, sending light through the curtains into the room. I read my own book for a few minutes and enjoyed the warmth of Ethan lying on my chest. It was probably my imagination, but it seemed our chests rose and fell in unison. I chuckled, thinking of a key item on Janet's Bill of Particulars against me was that I didn't like to cuddle. She was right. Other than for marital congress, I didn't like to be touched. Countless hours holding Ethan had broken down many of my physical barriers. I was becoming a convert.

The room darkened as the sky clouded over. I stared out the window for a few minutes. A large snowflake brushed against the glass, followed in short succession by several more. The wind picked up, and the windows rattled. I often wondered if our house had originally been a hunting shanty, with paper-thin walls, flimsy window frames, and rickety floors. Whoever converted it into a single-family home had made only cosmetic changes.

The house's ramshackle character was part of its appeal. Despite its flaws, guests reported it had a welcoming feel, warm and cozy, especially in the fall, when we spent a lot of time on the front porch or in the airy front room. Once winter descended, visitors often kept their coats on. Sometimes we jokingly suggested they stand outside against one of the house's walls to absorb the escaping heat. It wasn't too bad for Janet and me when we moved about in the house, generating our own heat. Otherwise, we mostly huddled together under blankets. Sometimes I felt like we were survivors of a plane crash who were lucky enough to stumble across an abandoned cottage. On particularly cold days, I imagined using sticks and rocks to construct a giant arrow in the front yard to point an air search team our way.

Lucky for us, Ethan didn't notice the cold. He slept with his hands exposed to the frigid air. Every time we covered them up, he wrestled them free from the blanket. I always found this baffling. Each time his little hands reappeared, it was like watching a jack-in-the-box pop up.

There was a lot I hadn't understood about babies before Ethan was born. Newborns made me extremely nervous. They seemed more like larvae than people; tiny, wrinkly masses of pink flesh over soft bone, curled up into little balls. Thankfully, when I was around another person's baby, there were always so many people competing to hold the child, I was able to appear gracious by deferring to others.

I tended to come on babies' radar screens after they left the larval phase. It wasn't that I finally sought their attention; I was still content to be merely a face in the crowd. But they often fixed their gaze on me and reached their arms toward me. With encouragement from jealous baby groupies, I held infants ever so briefly, then passed them off. After handing the bambino to an eager baby lover, the child often cried and reached for me. This was viewed as very charming by most. It didn't thrill me. The true fun for me began once babies started crawling and especially cruising.

My turning point with kids came one Sunday morning while visiting Janet's parents. Everyone left for church except for Janet, who remained behind to "help" me with our one-year-old nephew, Beksahn. She knew I was clueless about how to look after a child his age. To our mutual surprise, however, Beksahn only wanted to play with me. He and I set to work immediately.

There were still some cereal boxes and empty dishes left over from breakfast on the dining room table. I added more boxes of varying sizes and spread everything across the entire length of the table. With my hands firmly on his waist, he staggered across the table, leaving destruction in his wake. Cereal boxes tipped over, crashing on the table or onto the floor, spilling their contents everywhere. He laughed as his feet made crunching sounds on the cereal flakes. Bowls rattled wildly as his feet pushed them aside or off the table, where they made a delightful racket before finally coming safely to rest. After he made his way to the end of the table, I set him on the floor while I rearranged everything, and then lifted him back to the table so he could do it all over again. It was a blast. He was like Godzilla stomping through downtown Tokyo, though he laughed and smiled instead of breathing fire. *It would be cool if babies could breathe fire*, I thought as I pulled him off the table when Janet's family came through the door. Fortunately, they didn't mind the mess. My mother-in-law Aleta, like my own mom, valued creativity over tidiness.

At only five and a half months old on that cold February day, Ethan wasn't quite ready for those sorts of hijinks, but we were having a pretty good time together. Whenever his treatment schedule permitted, we walked around the neighborhood and visited with shopkeepers and passersby. At home, we lay side by side on the living room floor and read books and played with stuffed animals and little trucks. He tended to lie with his arms extended from his sides forming a cross and fingering a toy with one hand while he looked sideways at it. Several weeks before, he had dropped a toy soldier and pointed in the direction of the front door. There were no toys on that side of the room, so I wasn't sure what he wanted. But it gave me an idea.

I pulled the chairs away from the dining room table, put another blanket on the floor underneath it, and placed him there with a bunch of his toys. He smiled and kicked his legs. A draft from the front door prompted me to drape a couple of blankets over the table, completely enshrouding us in our own indoor tent. I propped up a lantern flashlight to illuminate the underside of the table, which reminded me of camping as a kid. I was even tempted to tell him ghost stories but decided against it, afraid it might come out in one of his therapy sessions as an adult.

We were under the table in our makeshift tent when Ethan's physical therapist, Julie, arrived at the front door. The three of us settled onto the living room floor, where it was easier for Julie to examine Ethan. After going through his history, medications, and basic care, she flipped him into different positions as if he were a human baton. I watched in awe of her strength and dexterity. Ethan was delighted. He smiled and laughed until she placed him squarely between her inner thighs, pressed her chest forward against his back, and hunched her shoulders around his arms, forcing his hands toward the center of his body. Wailing, he pushed back against her chest and desperately pressed his arms out against hers in vain. Julie showed considerable steeliness, firmly countering his efforts. I would have let him lie on his back again, where he seemed most comfortable.

She turned to me and explained that children who've had Ethan's kind of surgeries tend to lie on their backs with their arms extended to the side because they feel more stable that way. The problem with lying this way was he could only manipulate objects like toys with one hand. His development, she explained matter-of-factly, required he have his "hands to the midline with mutual fingering." I was momentarily distracted, repeating the odd-sounding phrase to myself, perhaps unconsciously trying not to face the life changes in the offing.

When she had my full attention, she said, "So, when he's not eating or sleeping, you must keep him in this position until he no longer tries to lie on his back with his arms extended."

I nodded, thinking I would need physical therapy myself afterward. She played with Ethan for a few more minutes in this awkward position, with him bawling the entire time. I admired her toughness. She seemed to be a very kind person, but she didn't flinch when it came to what she knew was best for Ethan.

After she left, I sat down next to Ethan with my legs splayed. He was on his back, his arms out to the side, with a toy in each hand. He looked at me and smiled. Watching him finger the toys, peering at one, then the other, down the length of each extended arm, I said, "I don't like that phrase, 'hands to the midline with mutual fingering,' anymore. Can we agree to stop using it?" He giggled and resumed playing.

I leaned back on my hands and sighed. "I'll figure something out, favorite guy," I said, and leaned forward to pick him up. I set him down between my legs, hunching my shoulders to force his arms forward. He squirmed and cried, pressing very hard against me. My mind raced as I tried to think about getting out of the house with the new care regimen. Images of different means of conveyance appeared before my mind's eye. A big red X flashed across each one, followed by an annoying buzzing sound to emphasize each one's unsuitability.

We weren't going anywhere that day or in the foreseeable future. Feeding, nap, and then holding him in this awkward position for the first half of the day, followed by feeding, nap, and holding him in the same awkward position again. It was the existential equivalent of directions on shampoo bottles stipulating a repeat wash. *If that didn't really produce über-clean hair, maybe I could also skip round two of Ethan's treatment?*

My right thigh cramped. Staring out the window, I was filled with self-pity as the rest of the world worked and played while we were trapped inside. The prospect of not leaving the house for who knew how long, Ethan and I pressed together the entire time even during naps, made me more sympathetic to my parents.

The year before Ethan was born, I had learned my parents had considered institutionalizing me after I had encephalitis. They had always told me the medical staff had suggested it, but eventually my parents had refused. Having a kid with seizures and wild mood swings who jumped up and ran down the street, trailed by parents, grandparents, and neighbors, made it too hard to maintain a regular social and family life.

"Were they planning this while they read me the funny papers and showered me with kisses?" I had asked Janet, who tried to console me.

The positive images in my mind—art projects with my mom and playing catch with my dad—were suddenly replaced by visions of Nurse Ratched lobotomizing me with an oversized hairpin while pitiless orderlies blasted me with a fire hose as I tried to squirm out of a straitjacket.

"You have got to be kidding," I imagined saying to my parents, by then already long dead. "Was it all so bad that you wanted to put me in some facility that would be the subject of a journalistic exposé one day? Really?"

My vision of parenting, however, was not all that different from my parents. An image of my mom and her beautiful, finely dressed friends, each holding a cigarette elegantly in one hand and a baby in the other, came to mind. If there were a caption, it might have read, "What's so hard about this?" My parents had more time before their parenting vision exploded. The second child by two years meant they'd had six relatively carefree family years before I developed encephalitis at age four, whereas my vision lasted only until Ethan was a couple of hours old. Still, we were birds of a feather in terms of not wanting to give up our former lives.

Fortunately for me, they decided not to institutionalize me. But being a kid with neurological problems was not easy. The extreme symptoms like seizures, slurred speech, and paralysis subsided. But I still had to contend with extreme nervous energy, anxiety, mood swings, poor auditory memory, a flash temper, and of course, the biggie, the sudden scrambling of my brain wave patterns. These residual effects didn't matter so much when you were off on a big adventure in Chicago, with no school, piano lessons, or church to sit through. I basked in the undivided attention of one or both parents, sometimes a grandparent to boot, or the unfailingly kind, under-standing hospital staff at Children's, where I was being treated as an outpatient.

Then, shockingly to me, at seven years old, after two and a half years in a kid lotus land, I was back home. I grinded it out with the other kid working stiffs; got up every day, went to school, sat still, and paid attention. Surrounded by kids, I became mostly invisible. I escaped notice except when called out for bad behavior.

"Just because you were sick all those years, young man, doesn't mean you can misbehave," I remember a teacher telling me. That recrimination was for my leg shaking uncontrollably during class.

As I got older, I learned to cope with exercise, mental stimula-tion, social interaction, and relaxation, all in the right amount at the appropriate time. My goal in life of simply having a good day made me sound easygoing, taking whatever came with a smile. But it wasn't so much that I lived in the moment as that I sought to control every moment. A typical day was divided into one-to-two-hour increments devoted to expending energy and occupying my mind. Through con-stant engagement of mind and body, I held myself together, accom-plished a fair amount, and had a lot of fun.

But now my fluidly rigid coping system faced its first true test. An irresistible force—my need for activity and stimulation—met an immovable object: our precious little boy's medical conditions.

My attention was drawn to Ethan pressing hard against my right side. He suddenly broke free and slid to my right, coming to rest with his shoulders against my thigh. Once settled, he extended his arms out to his side. Playing with a toy in his right hand, he stopped crying. The picture of contentment, he smiled and panted with excitement.

I sighed. Since Ethan was born, I'd gone from complete control to limited control to absolutely no control. I felt like I was about to step with Ethan through a portal into an unknown world. Encephalitis and CMT had forced me to continually adapt. It was kind of like having a secret life. No one really grasped what was involved in coping with them. What had sustained me was my determination to get as much out of life as I could, regardless of the circumstances. Now, I had to expand my personal bubble to include Ethan and put that spirit to work on his behalf. He had chosen me to take care of him, and I had agreed. The irresistible force had to team up with the immovable object, not work against it.

I touched his cheek gently with the back of my hand. "Okay, little guy. Let's assume the position." I lifted him up and placed him in front of me. "Doctor's orders," I added as I forced his arms forward. He cried and squirmed, but I remained firm.

After twenty minutes, I began to tire of the struggle and considered giving up. Staring at the sunlit opposite wall, I longed to get out for a walk. Suddenly, Ethan rested calmly against me. I glanced down to see him holding a toy over his shoulder. He was clearly handing it to me. It was very peaceful, wedged together like characters in an ancient myth who had become intertwined somehow and eventually became one being.

When he turned to look at me with a big smile, I imagined him thinking, *Isn't this great, Dad?*

"Yes, it is great, favorite guy," I said as I moved a few toys within his reach. "Sorry, Ted. We won't be making it in today after all."

6 Teeter-Tottering through Life

ETHAN AND I, JUST back from the playground, hung out in our backyard. After he cruised around an end table I'd made from a large tree stump, he pointed at the partially finished stone path. Ethan loved tools and was always interested in household projects, so I decided to lay a stone or two and let him help.

I set him down in the grass and gave him my torpedo level. He held it at arm's length and tipped each end up and down slowly, his eyes tracking the movement of the bubbles inside the fluid-filled chambers. I tapped his foot to get his attention and he handed me the level, which I placed on top of the stone. We crouched down together to check our work. Satisfied with the results, Ethan picked up a handful of sand and sprinkled it in the crevice between the stones, nodding at me afterward as he brushed off his hands.

"There's my little opera star." It was a neighbor in the alley with his dog. "I don't hear him anymore. How's he doin'? Everything okay?"

"Oh, yeah, we're great," I said. "It's the off-season. He's resting his voice."

He smiled and walked away. I gave Ethan a kiss and thought about how much I missed his voice chirping away much of the day. During his naps, I often worked in the backyard with the monitor nearby.

As he awakened, he performed the baby equivalent of vocal scales, which drew the attention of the alley denizens.

The early babbling began to include recognizable words when he was a little more than ten months old. Then, after his first birthday, the verbal tidal wave stopped.

Kristen, the speech therapist teaching him to swallow at the time, did an informal test. She sat behind him and beat a drum to get his attention. He didn't notice. It was as if she wasn't even there. We shared a moment of silence before she tried to reassure me by pointing out his great concentration and how he got so absorbed in what he was doing.

"Maybe he was just very focused," she said.

I appreciated her efforts. Yet there was no need for me to outsource wishful thinking. I did it instinctively. But even I conceded he had to be formally tested.

A month later, in the small, thickly insulated audiology testing booth at Children's Memorial Hospital, fifteen-month-old Ethan sat on Janet's lap, wearing earphones and holding a stuffed animal. On one wall was a large picture window that faced another small room with control panels, amplifiers, and sound equipment. The room was full of toys.

The audiologist, Dee, told Ethan to listen for sounds. If he heard one, he was supposed to turn toward it. If he turned in the right direction, boxes in the corners of the room would light up, and the monkey or bear inside would bang a drum or cymbal. Ethan was then to put the stuffed animal in a little container.

I voiced some concerns about the test design. Wouldn't a kid Ethan's age be inclined to play with a stuffed animal rather than give it up? Besides, with toys scattered throughout the small room, wouldn't he want to play with them rather than wait for a sound? And the hissing sounds produced in the earphones were almost identical to those made by our radiators at home, so he might simply perceive them as background noise.

Dee said that she and her colleagues would discuss my concerns. Then she nodded to a person on the other side of a large interior window to begin the test.

Ethan took the headphones off and fidgeted.

"He's a little tired," Janet explained apologetically before whispering in his ear, "Ethan, honey, please put the headphones on."

Still squirming, he shook his head before reaching for the container of stuffed animals.

After Janet put the headphones on him, we heard the hissing sounds through the earpiece on his left side. Ethan, busy turning the stuffed animal around in his hands, didn't look toward the sound. As the hissing sound began in the other earphone, he dropped the stuffed animal and tried to scoot down to the floor to explore toys in other parts of the room.

This went on for a while, with Ethan getting more and more frustrated at our attempts to get him to focus. Finally, after nodding to the person in the other room, Dee said, "This is clearly not going to work today since he can't sit still. We will have to schedule another test. Try to make sure he is more well rested next time."

Another test was scheduled for a week later. The second hearing test, like the first, was scheduled for 1:00 p.m., Ethan's naptime. Again, we left early in hopes he would nap on the way. Not a wink.

Before entering the testing room, Dee said, "I discussed your radiator theory with my colleagues. They all rejected it." Before I could respond, she added, "I also think it's a little crowded in the testing room. It would be better if you waited outside."

I tried to read or doze but instead ended up fuming about her parting advice after the first test. "Perhaps you should try to put him down for a nap a little earlier." *Does she think kids are like alarm clocks you can set?* And that bit about my "radiator theory" really got me into a lather, prompting me to mutter, "The scientific method requires that one consider alternative explanations, *n'est-ce pas?*"

The thickly insulated door of the testing room opened to reveal Dee beaming. I walked toward them, anxious about the test. *Was it possible the test went well? It must have, because Dee's smiling.* I began to hope.

Dee looked as if she was about to announce her engagement, not the results of a hearing test to worried, exhausted parents. I put my arm around Janet and tickled Ethan, who turned his head away while he let out a loud giggle. Dee was desperate to share with us the results of the test.

"He did great!" she said, pausing after each word, which she pronounced with special emphasis. Janet looked at me with surprise and relief. Even I, with my advanced capacity for self-delusion, felt a little surprised. But only for a moment. My crazy radiator theory was vindicated! All that worry for nothing! I let myself breathe for what felt like the first time in weeks. "He was a very good boy," Dee continued. "He sat very still and was very cooperative. We were able to complete the test."

We sat together at a nearby table. I was already thinking ahead to where we would have dinner to celebrate when Dee cut my musings short.

"We got great information," she said, still smiling. "There is no doubt. He has moderately severe sensorineural hearing loss."

I felt like I had been shrunk, then teleported into one of the bubbles floating in the torpedo level's liquid-filled chambers. I could see Dee's mouth moving, but I no longer heard what she said. I wasn't breathing, and my heart raced. Janet's face was turned toward Dee in disbelief. Dee pulled out some charts and graphs and pointed at dots along the curves. I struggled to speak. Eventually, I heard myself blurt out, "What? Sensorineural hearing loss? What's that?"

"Nerve damage," Dee said.

I was back in the soundproof bubble, this time voluntarily, like a cat climbing back in the carrier at the vet to avoid the exam. Janet and I sat numbly as Dee explained we would need to get clearance from an ENT specialist before getting Ethan fitted for hearing aids, and she ended the sentence with a cheerful rising pitch at the end. It was obvious she was well pleased with her work on this difficult case.

That night, I sipped a glass of wine while making dinner. I shook my head in disbelief that we hadn't seen this coming. The doctors in the NICU had told us hearing loss might be a complication of his treatment. His second major surgery as a newborn required that blood flow to his brain be cut off for twenty-two minutes while they widened a very narrow segment of his aorta. He had to take a heart medication called Lasix that was known to be associated with hearing loss.

Then there was the ventilator. Chances of hearing loss increased the longer he was on one. Standing at his crib in the NICU, waiting anxiously for Ethan's second surgery, I imagined a tag-team wrestling match of likely culprits in hearing loss. Baron von Lasix paired with the Ventilator versus the ever-shifty O2 Level and Panic Attack, famous for his harrowing blood pressure drop. As I began to worry less about one of them, another went on the attack.

Time on a ventilator as a possible cause especially gnawed away at me. After seven days, we were told, the likelihood of hearing loss increased greatly. Ethan had his first major surgery on Labor Day at just sixteen hours old. On the following Friday, his fifth day on a ventilator, his cardiovascular surgery was scheduled for 1:00 p.m., but the surgical team didn't arrive until 4:00 p.m. Dr. Backer said their first surgery of the day had taken much longer than anticipated. They were all exhausted and would rather do Ethan's surgery on Monday. However, they would go ahead with the operation if we wished.

An imaginary second hand pounded away in my head as he spoke. *Tick, tock, tick, tock, tick, tock.* "Get in there and fix him, you whiners!" I wanted to yell. But they looked so tired, it was crazy to expect them to go ahead with the surgery. As desperate as I was to get him off a ventilator, I realized we simply had to wait. They seemed relieved when I offered to buy them all a round of drinks instead.

After Ethan was released from the NICU at one month old, we were so overwhelmed with his care regimen that we mostly forgot about the possibility of hearing loss. Before he fell silent, I thought we had already experienced the worst and successfully climbed a steep rock face. We had no idea what we were doing at first. With no other choice, we worked our way slowly, steadily upward. Encountering new challenges like the laryngeal cleft was disheartening, but we backtracked a bit, moved a little sideways, and found alternate paths.

After almost a year of arduous climbing, we'd made it to the top. There was still a lot of work to do, such as unpacking our equipment and setting up camp. But soon our lives would be much like those who lived on a level surface. Or so we thought.

As unnerving as the heart issues had been, they would work themselves out. But hearing loss was a game changer. Although the holes in his heart wouldn't close, the heart itself would grow, making the holes relatively smaller over time. And his papery airways and flimsy esophagus might become firmer, making it easier for him to swallow and breathe. Even his G-tube would be removed soon, the little starburst-shaped scar the only reminder of his inability at birth to eat fully on his own. His hearing, though, would not improve; it would remain the same or get worse. The proverbial light at the end of the tunnel went dark.

"Nerve damage," I muttered in despair while I poured myself another glass of wine.

"What did you say, honey?" Janet asked from the entryway to the kitchen.

I was so lost in thought that I hadn't noticed her standing there and wasn't sure how long she'd been there.

"Nerve damage," I repeated as I leaned back against the table with tears welling up in my eyes. "It's hopeless. A no-win scenario. I can't take it."

Janet walked over and hugged me.

"The fact is," she said, "we just don't know yet. We'll have a better idea once we talk to ENT. Right now, let's focus on what's working well. You're usually a master at convincing yourself that everything is going to be okay. What's different about this?"

She was right. There might not really be a light at the end of the tunnel, but I certainly could imagine there was. I had dealt with my own "no-win" scenario for much of my life. Focusing on each and every day, not some imagined future, helped me cope with the residual effects of encephalitis and the degeneration of CMT. Maybe that approach would work with Ethan too.

I had to order his day in one-to-two-hour segments, as I did mine, shuffling the segments around to respond to different circumstances. This way I could make sure he received all the medical care he needed, including help with hearing loss, and fit in as much ordinary kid life as conditions permitted. In the long term, he had a good chance at being healthy and developing well. I was ready to work my way back up the rock face with Ethan.

A week later, we met with Dr. Young, the ENT specialist.

"What do you know about sensorineural hearing loss?" she asked as she looked up from the folder.

"Very little," Janet responded, "other than that it involves nerve damage."

"Not necessarily. Who told you that? I ask only," she said, "because we want to make sure that people are getting the right information."

Dr. Young jotted Dee's name down, then continued. "The problem is the cilia. They're hairlike fibers in the cochlea. Sometimes some or all of them die off. In Ethan's case, it appears to be only those in the higher frequency range. We can still correct for this with conventional hearing aids. We will continue to monitor his hearing closely to see if there is any further loss. If it remains as it is now, then it should be fully correctible. Because we caught it so early, his language skills should develop normally with speech therapy."

"Correctible"—my mantra from Ethan's first day! "That sounds positive," I said.

"Well, it is fortunate that the hearing loss is in the correctible range," she responded. "If his hearing worsens, we'll discuss other means of compensating for the loss."

Janet and Dr. Young talked some more about some very technical aspects of hearing loss and ways to respond to it. My mind drifted off to the old cliffhanger movies I'd watched as a kid, where cars came to a stop halfway over a huge drop-off. I imagined Ethan's condition teetering back and forth over the edge. More hearing loss might push him over the precipice into the uncorrectable range. What would we do then?

After our appointment with Dr. Young, hearing aids had to be ordered and earmolds made. Neither Janet nor I wanted to go through that with Dee, so Janet called the manager of the audiology department to request a different audiologist. Janet explained that dealing with Ethan's hearing loss was very emotionally difficult for us. Dee's insensitivity to our feelings made it hard for us to work with her going forward. The manager was very understanding. "I have the perfect person for you."

It took several weeks for the hearing aids to arrive and for earmolds to be made. In the interim, Ethan's G-tube was removed. We had assumed removal would require another surgery because his stomach was attached to his abdominal wall at the insertion point for the G-tube. But to our surprise, Dr. Luck said we could leave that in place and detach it only if other problems developed. So one morning, Kathy, Dr. Luck's unflappable nurse practitioner, pulled it out without any fuss. The site closed immediately like someone puckering their lips. It healed very quickly.

What a quality-of-life upgrade! The dry, chapped, irritated skin around the plastic tube had caused Ethan to flinch when he bent over or lay on his tummy. He now moved freely without pain. We no longer had to apply cream to the site, which was painful for him, or have the tube replaced when it leaked.

Several days after the G-tube was removed, we saw Kathy while at the hospital for a cardiology appointment. She knelt down to be eye level with Ethan. He grabbed her face with both hands and gave her a big kiss. He clearly felt life was looking up. I decided to try to channel some of his optimism. The glass now appeared to be half full.

The day finally arrived to pick up Ethan's hearing aids. Ethan's new audiologist, Stephanie, demonstrated how to set them up and make sure they were in his ears properly. High-pitched squeaking occurred when she flipped a switch on the back of each hearing aid.

"The squeaking indicates the earmolds are not completely in

place. Often you just need to coax them back in," she said, nudging each earmold a bit until the squeaking stopped.

"Hey, little buddy. How does that sound?"

He grinned, and his eyes lit up. He smiled at Stephanie and clapped his hands, listening with delight to each strike of his palms. It reminded me of the smiling little mechanical stuffed animals in the testing room that banged drums or crashed cymbals together. He was clearly elated.

Stephanie said we should gradually increase the amount of time he wore the hearing aids, so he could adjust to hearing a wider range of sounds more fully. Ethan, though, went from zero to sixty. He loved his hearing aids immediately and didn't object to wearing them, though it was hard to get earmolds to fit him properly. As he made his way around the house, the hearing aids tumbled off the delicate perch of his ears, squeaking loudly as they dangled by the cord attached to his shirt. His face shone brightly when we reinserted them. Even though I was skeptical they would ever stay in long enough to do him any good, I was relieved they didn't seem to bother him. The joyful way he experienced the world eased some of my apprehension about the future.

7 in-Flight Safety instructions

WHILE I GATHERED UP hearing aid equipment for an audiology appointment, three-year-old Ethan stood at attention, ready for inspection. He wore rain gear: hat, coat, boots—all plastic—and an umbrella. Except for the umbrella, which was tomato red, everything was blue, his favorite color at the time.

"You know, buddy," I said with a smile, "it's not going to rain today. Plus, it's going to be rather warm. I'm not sure that you'll need all that rain gear."

"Ethan need it," he said. "Rain forest today, Daddy. It rains a lot there."

The day before he'd been a mountain climber with ropes and a flashlight; the day before that, the scarecrow from *The Wizard of Oz*. Ethan was a serial obsessionist. Each day he assumed an entirely different persona. The one constant in the kaleidoscope of identity changes was me as equipment manager.

We arrived at the playground around 9:30 a.m. I scanned the crowd while Ethan played with the lock of the big metal gate. His usual MO when he didn't have a companion along was to shadow kids like a sheepdog, running around the perimeter, then work his way into their movements and become part of the flow. Before long, a kid would take notice and eventually play with him. With no kids his age there on this day, I knew I'd quickly be pressed into service.

Before I even put my bag down, he turned to me and said, "Come on, Daddy!"

He led me up the ramp and down the slides. If I got ahead of him, I lunged toward him roaring as he careened down the twisty slide or pretended to try to trip him as he worked his way back up the slide to the top.

Tiring of the chase, I positioned myself on a round, covered platform with a rope ladder in the center and a steering wheel on the wall. "Captain!" I shouted. "There's a storm coming our way. Should we prepare the sails?"

As he took the wheel and pretended to be buffeted by huge waves, I noticed another boy Ethan's age arrive and point us out to his mom. I was relieved to see her motion him toward us. He was quickly at our side, enabling me to slink away.

I sat down and scribbled in my notebook about something that had happened the day before at a beauty supply store. He and I were there to pick up a special order of two dozen boxes of toupee tape. At the counter, the clerk cast covert glances at me from different angles.

She finally said, "Your hair looks great. Do you mind if I ask where you got it?"

She turned beet red when I explained we used the tape to hold Ethan's hearing aids in place and apologized over and over while I tried to reassure her I was not offended.

"Here's to you, toupee tape," I muttered as I watched Ethan and his new chum chase each other around the playground with Ethan's hearing aids firmly in place.

After about an hour, the challenge was disengagement. I had to reenter the fray. I approached them yelling, "Pirates are boarding the ship. Run!" A chase ensued. They ran faster and climbed more quickly. They expended considerable energy looking over their shoulders and laughing. After ten minutes or so, I called out to them. "Boys, I need a break. You are too fast for me." I was truly a little breathless.

"Yeah, you not catch us, Daddy!" Ethan shouted, breathing hard. He repositioned one of his hearing aids that had worked its way atop one of his ears.

We said goodbye to Ethan's playmate and left for our 11:00 a.m. audiology appointment. The speedup session had served its purpose. It wore Ethan down enough that he was willing to leave the playground without a fuss. He was happy to sit in the stroller, chattering away for the three-block walk to the hospital.

It was 10:45 a.m. when we reached the lobby. This gave Ethan time to play with the interactive kid displays and for me to pick up an iced mocha at the coffee shop in the corner. Trailing him from one display to the next, I sipped my coffee and responded to his ongoing commentary. Between queries and excited musings, I daydreamed about how I was going to get a little shut-eye.

I was always on the prowl for a suitable nap spot, and they were everywhere for someone with my napping dexterity. I could fall asleep without difficulty in the most uncomfortable positions—in moving or parked cars, doctors' offices, on park benches, even during yoga classes. The final resting pose was a given, of course, but I had even dozed during nonresting poses.

The importance of naps for me was not lost on Ethan. While visiting his grandparents, he had constructed a nice little cabin out of Lincoln Logs. A figure stood in an upright position on the outside, while another lay prone on the floor inside. Grandma asked him who the figures were, and he responded that the one on the outside was Mommy on her way to work. And the figure inside the house?

"That's Daddy," he said. "He needs a blanket and pillow."

Our yearlong experiment in sleep deprivation began shortly after his second birthday when Ethan had stopped eating much solid food and mostly consumed chocolate milk and decaffeinated iced mochas. Dr. Holinger found a dime wedged vertically at the surgical site, where Dr. Luck had repaired his esophagus as a newborn. We were embarrassed that it could have been there for perhaps two months before we suspected something was stuck in his throat.

To our surprise and relief, Dr. Holinger and his staff didn't alert child welfare authorities. Instead, they defended us, explaining how sometimes food could pass unhindered because he was often able to cough up anything that got stuck. We wouldn't know if something was lodged there. Our embarrassment only grew when Ethan asked for a decaf iced mocha after waking up from surgery. The crowd of doctors, nurses, residents, and medical students around Ethan's bed laughed and agreed that an iced mocha would have been nice right then.

Because the scar tissue in his esophagus did not grow normally, it had to be stretched surgically in a procedure called a dilation. It wasn't one and done, unfortunately. The scar tissue could be stretched only a little at a time, so between Thanksgiving and mid-January we took Ethan to Children's at 5:30 a.m. for a dilation twice a week.

The outpatient surgical center became our home away from home. We got to know the staff and shared jokes and personal stories. Ethan padded around in his Elmo slippers holding a stuffie. He explored the surroundings and exchanged greetings with patients and the staff. Before putting him under each time, Dr. Holinger showed him the instrument used to stretch the scar tissue. After carefully eyeing the round metal band and various other equipment, Ethan nodded with a smile that he was ready for the anesthesia. Afterward, we visited some more, and Ethan was treated with popsicles.

The downside, of course, was that the surgeries wreaked havoc on our schedule. Getting him up at an ungodly hour wouldn't have been a problem if he had his usual nap in the early afternoon. The problem, though, was he slept midmorning for quite a while under anesthesia, which left him groggy and listless for the next several hours. Spending much of the afternoon slumped in a kiddie Barcalounger, dozing on and off, he roused around dinner time, stayed up late, and woke up early the next day. He was revved up and going full steam all day without a nap until the next dilation.

The pace of dilations slowed down over the winter when Ethan developed frequent pneumonias. Wracked with a dry, unproductive cough, he struggled to breathe. To prevent him from aspirating, Janet and I held him upright in a chair all night. I did the weekday nights, and she did the weekend ones. It was cozy, being pressed together all night, but none of us got a full night's sleep. The oral steroids he took to reduce inflammation in his lungs helped him breathe easier. Their side effect, however, was considerable nervous energy and irritability. Suddenly, calm, sweet Ethan became Steroid Boy. He tore around frantically, not napping and still sleeping fitfully at night with one of us in the chair, because the cough continued, though in diminished form. When he finally recovered, he had another dilation, followed by another pneumonia, on and on. The Greek god Hypnos at Hera's request could induce Zeus to sleep; our appeals went unanswered.

I was desperate for sleep when we checked in for his appointment. My body ached, my head throbbed—even my eyes hurt. It was like something inside me was trying to get out, pressing against all my joints. Only sleep would calm the beast and relieve the internal pressure. Much more was at stake than my comfort level. The pressure in my head, what Janet once aptly described as the big squeeze, suggested a phase shift loomed ahead, that bizarre, momentary disconnect with my own mind and body. I hadn't had one since Ethan was born, which was surprising given the stress of managing his care. Lately, though, being so exhausted, I thought for sure one would occur. For Ethan's sake, I wanted to avoid one. Getting a nap seemed like a matter of life and death.

We headed for the car after Ethan's audiology appointment while Ethan prattled on about robots. I ran down my options for both of us getting a nap. The easiest one was to let him fall asleep in the car. I could pull off into the lakefront park and settle into a nice snooze myself.

Sadly, a bizarre incident the previous winter suggested the lakefront was a nap-free zone. Both of us had been sound asleep in the car. Suddenly, I was awakened by a loud tapping sound. Startled, I looked over wide-eyed at someone standing at the driver's side window.

"Are you okay?" he asked. "Are you both okay?"

I nodded, a little bewildered, as I watched him run down the path. He must have thought it was a murder suicide. It almost was . . . killing him for waking us up, and killing myself in despair about not getting a nap.

Now, I mulled over other options. I could drive straight home and let Ethan fall asleep along the way, pull into the garage, open the windows, and turn off the car. With the big side doors open, he might continue to sleep comfortably. With the warm weather, however, our neighbors would be on their back porch watching TV. It would be hard for me to fall asleep listening to Jerry Springer at high volume. And if the Cubs were playing, they would be screaming at the screen.

If he fell asleep on the way home, I could try to pick him up, carry him inside, and let him sleep on the couch or ideally upstairs in his bed. This often worked when he had been sleeping normally. In his current state, though, I wasn't confident I could get him inside without him waking up.

The most difficult option was the only realistic one. I had to somehow keep him awake during the ride home. I set him in his seat, gave him some yogurt, and opened the trunk to see what I had to keep him busy. I was in luck. There was a Power Ranger. Concerned that it was still not enough, I resumed rummaging. Our trunk was an automobile version of Mary Poppins's bag. I found a bag of chocolate coins underneath some beach toys.

"Ohhh," I said, as though I'd stumbled upon a long-lost family heirloom. "Thank you, Lord."

I put the Power Ranger and the coins on the front seat where he couldn't see them and drove off down the street. Ethan paged quietly through a comic book, then stared out the window. Sensing that he could drop off at any moment, I handed him the Power Ranger when we stopped at Belmont and Sheffield.

His eyes lit up, and he talked excitedly. First an inventory. "Charlie has my green Power Ranger, and I have Tommy's red one. Tommy has my blue Power Ranger. The blue one is the best. Did you know that?"

"I do now," I said, wondering how much sleep the average Power Ranger got each day.

"The blue one is an S.P.D. Ranger."

"Is that better?" I asked. I knew the answer; I wanted to keep him talking.

"Yeah," he said, looking out the window.

"Why is it better?" I inquired with a quizzical look.

A truck went by his open window, so he didn't hear me. He turned back toward me and opened a new topic—acquisitions. After a quick summary of what he and his friends wanted to get, he said, "Tommy has a purple Shadow Ranger."

"Shadow Rangers? That sounds bad. Are they bad guys?" I asked.

He exploded with excitement. He listed the various colors, outlined their capacities, and described the manifold threats they posed to decent citizens everywhere. The Power Rangers, thankfully, remained steadfast, our last line of defense.

As we drove along the cemetery north of Irving Park, the talking tapered off, and he stared silently out the window. When his eyes started to droop, I put the bag of chocolate coins in the small storage compartment between the two front seats and called his attention to them by rooting around inside. "Where is that darn hand sanitizer?" I said in a stage whisper.

He noticed the bag of coins as we slowed to a stop at Lawrence Avenue. His eyes widened as he blurted out, "Can I have one?"

"One what?"

"The gold thing. Can I have one, please?"

"What thing, buddy?"

"Right there," he said, leaning forward pointing. "The chocolate!"

The seat belt and shoulder harness prevented him from jumping to the floor to tear the bag open. "Oh, you mean these coins?" I asked as the light changed.

"Yeah. Can I have one? Please!"

"Sure, feller once we get to another stoplight."

At Foster Avenue, I pretended I couldn't get the bag open.

"Please, Daddy, please, can I have one?"

"Here, I almost have it," I said, relieved when the light changed. "Oh, bummer. We'll have to wait for the next light, Ethan. Sorry."

I'm going to pay for this in hell, I thought, as I saw an angel statue outside the garden store.

I sighed as we stopped at a light a few blocks from our house. Handing him a coin, I relished his look of delight as he unwrapped it and popped it in his mouth. *Did you see that, angel? See how happy he is? Surely that counts for something?* Turning onto our street, I gave him another one.

"Thanks, Daddy," he said.

I busied myself with silent self-praise as we walked into the house. A rare golden moment of controlled sleep disruption. You keep your child awake—using the gentlest of means—long enough to get home for a proper nap. No tapping, poking, and prodding. Giving him a chocolate coin wasn't even a bribe in a strict sense, I told myself, though I would have been hard-pressed to justify that claim.

The hypocrisy was harder to explain away. What could be more comforting than a quick snooze in the back of a moving car? Me of blanket-and-pillow fame could certainly attest to that. Yet the person he trusted most the most in the world was trying to keep him awake, so that this trusted person could get some sleep. On airplanes, parents were instructed to put their oxygen masks on before helping their children with theirs. Didn't that same logic apply to naps? Putting our stuff down inside, I asked him to go to the bathroom.

"No, Ethan want cookie."

Oh, man. This does not bode well.

"Go to the bathroom, and we will eat a cookie while we read books," I said.

He shook his head violently and kicked his feet. "No read books, no read books, watch moody!"

I stormed out of the room, calling back over my shoulder, "Fine. Have it your way." He continued kicking the floor and shaking his head. I went to the bathroom while the protest continued.

I came back into the front room with a new proposal. "Okay, we watch *part* of a movie *after* your nap. First, though, we read a couple books."

We trudged up the stairs and settled into the reclining chair in his room and began reading. It was a rather busy book, not particularly interesting. Suddenly, he hopped up and scooted around the corner. I called out to him, "Let's read some more stories." No answer. "Do you want to go straight to bed?" Silence. I got up and searched for him. He was in the closet behind the door to the upstairs deck, smiling.

"Let's go to bed," I said, carrying him back to his room.

He fell asleep immediately. I plopped onto our bed, closed my eyes, and started to drift off. I was pulled back to consciousness, however, when he began chattering in his room. There were sounds of things dropping on the floor, followed by silence. *Okay, everything's fine. Just relax.* A few minutes passed with me staring at the ceiling. I heard the headboard of his bed bang against the wall and a few words that I couldn't quite make out. I craned my neck to look over toward his room, hoping, in my distress, to send a relaxation beam in his direction. The ruckus stopped. *It worked*, I thought, a bit surprised and intrigued. *I should use relaxation beams more often.* Then I heard a very quiet whimper. I decided to try to ride it out. Absent distressed calling out or intense crying, I saw no reason to intervene.

He upped the ante. "Help me!" he called out. "Help me, Daddy." *Okay*, I sighed, *that was addressed specifically to me.* I had to go. He had somehow gotten one of his feet caught in the small gaps in the back bed rail.

Once he was freed, he dropped down in a crouched position and said, "Sorry," into his pillow.

"It's fine," I said, still annoyed. "Please try to go to sleep."

"Okay," he said. He dropped down from his crouched position and laid his face down on his bed. Turning his head up from his pillow, he said, "Mommy and Daddy's bed, sleep in Mommy and Daddy's bed."

We didn't get that far, collapsing together in the reclining chair in his room. He was pantless, holding a papier-mâché chair in one hand and an empty DVD box in the other. Despite the heat, I grabbed a blanket, and we settled into a very warm cuddle. I craned my neck to accommodate his long frame, astonished at how much he'd grown. He was breathing very deeply. I looked down at him, then drifted off to sleep.

About an hour later, I woke up to the sound of our dog barking loudly in the hallway. *How did he get inside?* "Wait a minute," I muttered. *We don't have a dog.* The barking was from the neighbor's terrier in the passageway between the two houses, the sound wafting up through the open window in our hallway.

Still groggy, covered in perspiration, I wrapped the blanket more tightly around us. With my chin resting on Ethan's golden mop of hair, I drifted back to sleep.

8 Cat without a Name, Cell without a Number

I TRIPPED OVER SYLVESTER while rushing out the front door. He batted his paws frantically at the mouse that got away.

"Oh, fuck! You have got to be kidding me!" I yelled.

Late Friday afternoon, I was rushing to get our application to the adoption agency before it closed for the day, and Sylvester, the hapless hunter, had brought a mouse *into* the house. I opened the door in hopes that he would run outside with his prize, but he had already lost track of it. Sylvester and I both searched in vain for a couple of minutes before leaving the house together empty-handed. I turned the documents in with only seconds to spare.

I picked Ethan up at his friend Charlie's house and told him the story on the way to meet Janet at the Edgewater Lounge. He laughed so hard he was crying. Over dinner, the three of us reviewed Sylvester's antics.

The consensus favorite was the "where's kitty cat" game. Ethan and I, joined over time by an ever-growing number of kids and adults, walked up and down the sidewalks and alleys, watching for Sylvester to appear. He'd surface on the top of a fence, on some garbage cans, on the roof of someone's porch, each time disappearing for a minute or two before he popped up again somewhere else to squeals of delight.

The ever-social Sylvester, who we believed was the same age as Ethan, three and a half, endeared himself to people throughout the neighborhood. We received regular reports about him stopping by their homes to sun himself or to have a snack. He even followed us into parties on occasion, working the crowd for affection or a treat or to find a nice spot for a nap. At a gathering the previous week, a group of kids of varying ages dashed out onto the back porch. They were breathless with excitement. "Snowvester's up on Jennie's bed!" little Katie reported. Indeed, there he was, sitting regally on the bed like he owned the place.

Sylvester was essentially a feral cat with indoor privileges. We had adopted him the previous fall. Sylvester had wandered into a camp-ground in western Michigan run by friends of ours. He created quite a stir and always found his way into the center of every group activity. He also slept around, literally, staying in a different tent every night until the camp closed in the fall.

Not being "cat people," we polled feline-loving friends on whether Sylvester should be an indoor or outdoor cat. It was a landslide in favor of the former. Sylvester voted with his feet by positioning himself out of sight, then streaking out the door when we came in or out. After we were more on guard, he went for the nuclear option of escaping by ripping holes in the window screens.

"Look!" two-year-old Ethan had exclaimed one morning, pointing at the back deck. "Sylbetter out dere." Sylvester had recreated the conditions of the summer camp, where he could come and go as he pleased.

By Sunday afternoon, we became worried when he had not made an appearance since the comical mouse-in-the-house incident. Ethan and I tied notices to trees throughout the neighborhood. "Lost cat/ large black-and-white male/very friendly/named Sylvester." It took us most of the afternoon to post the notices, partly because Sylvester's territory was so large but also because we were stopped innumerable times along the way by Sylvester fans, who expressed their concern and shared stories about him. He was beloved.

As his handler and home care nurse, my take on Sylvester was not quite as positive. Sylvester often got in fights with other cats and sometimes even raccoons, forcing me to rush outside at all hours to intervene. Afterward, Sylvester would have to be kept indoors for a while to recover from his wounds. He hobbled behind me the entire day, giving me the "what-for" look. He also blamed me for inclement weather. Apparently, feeding him and operating the doors gave him the impression that everything else was under my control as well. I even got yelled at regularly about Sylvester following us around the neighborhood. "Don't you know that cat should be inside?" As if I had some say in that.

I kept all this to myself, however, because Ethan loved Sylvester with all his heart. They were nice companions. When Ethan set up trains or worked on a project, Sylvester sat at his feet watching him or placing his paw on something Ethan was reaching for. Ethan would tell Sylvester about his day, some book he was reading, or the latest toy or game he found absorbing. He also consulted with Sylvester about his paintings, going over color options or the basic concept of the piece.

"This one is about Mommy and me enjoying chocolate in a beautiful land," he explained to Sylvester, who looked up at him, then down at the painting, before putting a paw on one edge that was bent upward.

Ethan was convinced that Sylvester understood him.

"There is like a person in there," he said to me a few months before Sylvester's disappearance. I nodded, amused by the thought of the old sitcom *Bewitched*—poor Darrin Stephens changed into Sylvester by his mother-in-law.

Their relationship was perhaps what God had in mind when, after noting it was "not good for the man to be alone," he created the animals in hopes of finding a "fitting helper" for Adam. I chuckled at the image of Yahweh as a struggling parent like me trying to do what he thought best for his progeny yet missing the mark because he did not fully understand Adam. There was so much I didn't understand about Ethan or people in general. Still, I was convinced that as much as he loved Sylvester, it was clear Ethan, like Adam, longed for someone like him as a life companion. He desperately wanted a sibling to shower with love.

We tried to provide him one. We wanted a crowded house, many voices, constant movement. Chaotic, yes, but to us that seemed natural. Would it be more difficult? Of course, in some respects. Money would be tighter, there would be scheduling problems, conflicts and rivalries would occur. We didn't overlook or discount any of these possibilities. Yet such problems were often surmountable. Loneliness, though, was harder to remedy. Ethan had cousins and was adept at establishing and maintaining relationships. He very probably would find love and be part of communities that would sustain him emotionally.

However, there was something different, emotionally deeper, more permanent about the relationship with a sibling. As loving as our relationship with him was, he wanted someone whom he could share things with that he was not comfortable sharing with us. And we weren't getting any younger. Already in our mid-forties, it was reassuring to think a brother or sister might be there with him once we were gone. To paraphrase Genesis, it was not good for the boy to be alone.

Two heartbreaking miscarriages later, we decided to adopt a baby. Seitzer-Smith family standard operating procedures were initiated. We talked and talked about options, what we would like to do, what it would be like, without actually nearing a decision or taking any action. If not for one of Ethan's godmothers, Ruth, we would still be at that stage.

"This just will not do," she said. "You have to get moving."

At her insistence, we finally set to work, selected an option, and filed documents. In six months, if all went according to plan, Ethan would have a baby sister from China.

Right then, though, we had a more immediate concern. Sylvester was still missing. By the time we got home late Sunday afternoon, the phone constantly rang with reports of Sylvester sightings. Early Monday morning, we received a very promising, though disturbing, tip from our neighbor Sidni from across the alley, who had seen someone picking Sylvester up.

"I think I know who has your cat," she said over her back fence. "While I was walking my dogs on Saturday afternoon, I noticed Sylvester at the end of my block on the opposite side of the street lounging on the large stone ledge near the steps to someone's porch. Nothing unusual there. But when I returned home some time later, I saw someone lean over and try to pick him up. You should be concerned," she said with her head tilted back a bit and one eyebrow raised slightly, "for this person makes it her mission in life to take in stray cats." She continued in a measured tone to emphasize each word, "And she has a pretty broad definition of stray cats. She doesn't think cats should be outside and believes that any cat she finds outdoors is lost and needs to be rescued."

After dropping Ethan off at art camp, I went over to the suspected catnapper's house. One of our notices was strung around a tree out front. The house was dark with thick curtains covering all the windows, and the front door had something attached to the back side, so that it was hard to see in through the glass panels.

I rang the doorbell several times but never heard it ring. After knocking on the door, first softly, then progressively harder, I was about ready to leave a note when a late-middle-aged woman came around the side of the house.

"What do you want?" she asked, wearing an apron and holding a shovel.

"I'm sorry to bother you," I began. "But someone said that you might have found our cat. He is a large, friendly, black-and-white male tuxedo cat."

She gestured with her head and walked toward the backyard with me close behind. A tree on the left side of the patio gave it a very enclosed feel. A dog barked inside the house, which drew my attention briefly to a storage area crammed with stuff under the back porch. Over her shoulder I noticed the garage door open. I wondered if that's where she had Sylvester.

I felt uneasy as she began quizzing me about Sylvester. "How long has he been gone?" she asked, looking at me with squinted eyes.

"We believe since Friday evening," I answered.

"Well, I found a cat down at the corner of my block on Saturday, so he's clearly not yours," she said without explaining how she had come to that conclusion.

"He might be, though," I answered, "because someone reported seeing him down the street from you."

She pounced on this like a detective who caught a suspect in a misstatement. "How could you not know how long he's been gone? Don't you take care of him?"

"He's an outdoor cat," I responded, a bit embarrassed that I didn't know for sure how long he'd been gone. "He will be outside for extended periods in the summer," I added, feeling defensive.

"How does he eat if he doesn't come in frequently?" she asked.

She was close to getting a confession. "Some of the neighbors feed him. He's a very social cat."

She gave me a disapproving look. Her suspicions about me as an unsuitable cat owner were no doubt confirmed. Clearly, I wasn't getting anywhere with her. And I was also becoming a little worried I might end up in a crate in the garage or in the storage area. I tried to move things forward by asking, "Can I see him please?"

"Well," she said hesitantly, "he is inside. Let me get his collar."

His collar? I thought. *Why not let me see him? And how did he have his collar on but not his tag?* The fact was, we didn't often see his collar. It was usually so buried in his shaggy mane that we rarely even knew it was missing until we saw it on our front porch. Neighbor kids often tossed it there after finding it hanging from a fence, in their backyard, or in the alley somewhere. But the tags had never come off without the collar. *Did she take the tags off?*

She came back and thrust a badly worn collar through the small opening in the back door. "Is this his collar?" she asked.

"Yes, I believe it is," I answered, though I really wasn't sure.

She looked at me for a second, tilted her head toward me, and said, "Well, this isn't your cat. I know your cat. I've seen him around here for about a year. He won't come anywhere near me."

I can't imagine why.

"This cat was crying on a porch on the corner," she said. "He came right up to me and rolled over, exposing his belly for me to pet him."

Sylvester's signature move.

"No, no, this cat is much larger than your cat, and he hasn't eaten in two days."

A feline hunger strike.

I was about to ask her to explain why that proved it was not Sylvester when she said, "And this one isn't dingy around the paws like your cat."

Okay, now it's getting personal. I was exasperated. It was almost time to pick Ethan up, so I needed to make an exit. I said, "Well, I'm pretty sure it's our cat. I'll have my wife come back with pictures."

I walked away thinking we would need to rescue Sylvester in a dramatic predawn raid. I wondered if I could buy tear gas in the city. *Probably not. I would have to go to the suburbs for that.*

Ethan and I spent the afternoon in the backyard rather than shopping for combat gear. First, Charlie and his little brother Henry came over, and the three of them played in the pool for a couple hours. Joey filled the late-afternoon shift, which centered around medieval knights battling for control of an elaborate sandcastle surrounded by moats. Joey ambled down the front walk with his mom and two brothers as Janet came up the block from the other direction.

Over dinner we discussed our options. Janet, who was not an early riser, did not support a paramilitary operation in the wee hours of the morning. She opted instead for another attempt at persuasion, bravely taking the photo album with her to try to win Sylvester's release.

She returned about forty-five minutes later with Sylvester meowing loudly inside the cat carrier. We let him out. He quickly set to work trying to settle onto Ethan's lap. After fussing over Sylvester for a while, Janet explained that everything went much as it had for me until she passed her the photo album of Sylvester.

"I waited nervously," Janet reported. "A few minutes passed. I was worried she wouldn't give me the album back, let alone Sylvester. The jailer returned, passed the album back, and said, 'I'll bring him down, but it's still not your cat.' When she returned, I couldn't see Sylvester. But he started to crow when I said, 'Is that you, Sylvester? My little darling, is that you?' He immediately set in to complaining. '*Rup, rup, rup.*'"

"I smiled down at Sylvester," she continued. "He poked his head up through the opening. I scratched his head while he continued his tongue-lashing. The jailer was willing to let him go, but not without a diatribe about outdoor cats. I walked down the stairs with Sylvester's loud meowing drowning out her closing arguments."

Ethan sat with Sylvester on his lap while Janet went inside to get him some food. Sylvester jumped off his lap when Janet returned. Ethan crouched down to pet him while he ate.

"Thanks, Mom," Ethan said, giving her a hug. "It's great having Sylvester back. I would miss him so much if he were gone all the time."

Janet gave him a kiss. He and I followed her into the house, leaving Sylvester outside where he clearly belonged.

9 Mr. Rogers to the Rescue

I OPENED MY EYES and looked around the room. Something had changed, but I couldn't put my finger on it. Four-year-old Ethan and I were still pressed together in a reclining chair with his head wedged under my chin. It suddenly struck me. He had stopped coughing.

What a relief. Ethan's dry, unproductive cough was so painful for him. It filled us with dread, partly because we could do very little to help him but also because we feared it might result in a severe pneumonia. It occurred to me that the absence of sound was like an event itself worthy of celebrating, like when the bombing stops in an air raid. The war might not be over, but you could still enjoy the pause in the fighting.

It was a short celebration. Only time would tell whether he aspirated significantly overnight. Esophagi are miraculous organs. They flex frequently to push acid and food particles back down into the stomach, one of many autonomic functions taking place all the time in our digestive tract. Like many TEF kids, however, the muscles lining Ethan's esophagus were rather weak, so they were often overmatched by the ever-assertive stomach acid. The laryngeal cleft was the anatomical equivalent of leaving the barn door open. Coughing fits produced a stampede of reflux toward the opening. We slept in the chair together in hopes that gravity would slow down the rush for the door.

An hour later, Ethan sat in his kiddie Barcalounger and watched an episode of *Mr. Rogers' Neighborhood* in which someone explained how a conveyor belt operated to the enraptured Mr. Rogers. Kneeling at Ethan's side, preparing oral syringes, I recalled the terror I felt the last time he had such a night six weeks ago. When I had set him in the chair then, he'd immediately slumped down and tilted to one side as though he had no bones or muscle. Placing his little hand on my knee, he said, "Help me, Daddy, please help me."

Now downstairs, Ethan played quietly with toy cars on the kitchen floor while I made the call.

"Who was that?" he asked, after I gave him some Tylenol for his rising fever.

"That was Dr. Green's office."

"Will Dr. Green take my cold away, so I can breathe?"

"Yes, but not right away."

"I know. But I'm sick."

I found it interesting that he added the word "but," as though I doubted him. Continuing to press his case, he said, "I'm worse today."

I thought so too. Watching for symptoms of pneumonia was like being a character in a vampire movie. You needed to be ready, stake in hand, to see if someone bitten turned into a vampire. But in lieu of a stake, I had the pulmonary department on speed dial.

Ethan assembled a new toy robot in the back seat on the way to Children's while I thought about our struggle against pneumonia over the previous eighteen months. We knew his rickety ductwork made it hard for him to swallow without aspirating. And yet we still were taken by surprise when he started to develop pneumonia halfway through his third year. In our defense before the cosmic parenting control board, which was in permanent session in my imagination, I would say we could handle only so much at a time. The recurrent respiratory infections began in the midst of a long series of surgeries on his esophagus, which were also unanticipated (by us). *Oh, well*, I thought, glancing at Ethan playing so cheerfully, *we should cop a plea and be done with it.*

After parking on a side street near the hospital, I rapped my knuckles on the dashboard thinking that at least we no longer had to jump through so many hoops to get him the help he needed. Early on in Ethan's respiratory trials, I had taken him to the pediatrician first, who, understandably concerned about Ethan's dropping O2 levels, wanted to send him to the ER in an ambulance. Painful memories of an ambulance debacle when Ethan was three months old prompted me to insist on driving him myself. The stalemate was resolved each time when the pulmonary staff at Children's persuaded the pediatrician to let me drive him to the hospital. After several iterations, we set up a protocol. I called the pulmonary staff directly when Ethan had a fever after a night of coughing, and we went straight to the pulmonary department at the hospital.

While I checked in with the receptionist, Nurse Sadia knelt down to say hello to Ethan and listened attentively as he told her about the features of a robot toy he held in the crook of his arm. His newfound perkiness suggested the Tylenol was taking effect.

She turned to me and with a cheerful smile asked how I was doing. We chatted for a moment.

I was genuinely relieved to be in the hospital but not only because Ethan would get the care he needed. The hospital was a safe zone for me too. It was a little awkward as a stay-at-home dad being the only guy in a sea of women. Surrounded by people not making eye contact was kind of like being at a nude beach; I didn't know where to direct my gaze. The norms of expected behavior were also unclear. I considered it polite to say hello while passing someone on the sidewalk or standing next to them at a playground. It was also easier. Looking away or pretending someone was not there required more effort, although it was standard practice. I should have been accustomed to this, having spent years as a graduate student at the University of Chicago, where such deliberate nonresponsiveness was known as "the Fifty-Seventh Street salute." Now, it was a little dispiriting, since this was the only adult contact I had much of the time.

At the hospital, by contrast, I always appeared in the visible light spectrum. It was safe to say hello because I was certain the staff would respond or at least not look away as if I were not there. As Janet pointed out, the staff realized dealing with kids was different. Parents were emotionally fragile and needed reassurance. Saying hello, asking how one was doing, and sharing personal stories meant a lot to people who were a little traumatized.

In an examination room, we formed a little assembly line. I put a Transformer on the chair next to me; Ethan grabbed it and placed it on the window ledge behind the chair. Once he began arranging them in different configurations, I occupied myself with self-doubt about his condition. Seeing him goof around with Nurse Sadia had made me wonder if it were a false alarm.

Stacy, the nurse practitioner, popped in for a brief preliminary exam, followed a few minutes later by Dr. Green. Ethan picked his head off my chest, looked directly at Dr. Green, and smiled broadly. Watching them chat about the ups and downs in the world of Transformers, I was suddenly struck by how much they both reminded me of my dad. They had physical similarities, such as long appendages, slender frames, and erect bearing, but even more was their calm, cheerful dispositions and complete lack of vanity. When you were with my dad, it was like you were the only person in world. I got that impression of Dr. Green as well.

"He sounds pretty good," Dr. Green said, lifting the stethoscope from Ethan's chest. "A bit of coarseness, though. The fever after a night of coughing is a bad sign. Let's have him get a chest X-ray."

The X-ray revealed that Ethan had yet another pneumonia. Fortunately, it was a mild one, which could be treated at home with antibiotics and steroids.

Ethan slept blissfully as I carried him to the car. As I strapped him into his seat, he opened his eyes to tiny slits and said, "Thanks, Dad, it was good seeing Dr. Green. Will he take my cold away?"

"He will, favorite guy," I responded. "But you should sleep now."

He closed his eyes and rested his right temple against the headrest. We were parked on a quiet, leafy street south of the hospital. His prescriptions wouldn't be ready for a while, so I put the seat back, opened the front windows, and drank the coffee still left in my thermos. As I enjoyed the sound of birds singing in the trees and kids frolicking on a nearby playground, I thought about the pulmonary staff. Ethan loved all his doctors. In fact, he found something to love in everyone. But lately he seemed to have a special rapport with the pulmonary staff. I concluded it was because he associated them with release from terror. While he was hospitalized for pneumonia in a severely weakened state, as he had been six weeks before, the attending physicians must have appeared like apparitions to him. He typically saw Stacy and Dr. Green once he was well on the way to recovery, in the full light of day, a new dawn of breathing easier.

I finished my coffee. Glancing in the rearview mirror, I noticed Ethan was awake. Our eyes met; we both smiled.

"Hi, Dad," he said. "I'm going to sleep some more." I nodded, but he was already asleep again.

I unlatched my seat to bring it back upright, but it lurched too far forward. Before I could reposition myself, my diaphragm pressed against the hard edge of the steering wheel. The brief moment of pain reminded me of sitting in a straight-backed chair with Ethan during that severe pneumonia a month and half earlier, when the metal top of the chair pressing against my upper back felt like someone was slowly cutting into me with a dull knife.

That was a real first for me. During the countless hours I had spent holding Ethan, I would have done anything to relieve my discomfort. Then, though, it was simply out of the question. Struggling to remain motionless, I was suddenly struck by how badly I had misunderstood Janet's feelings after Ethan was born. I was completely puzzled by her refusal to pass him off, even for a moment, so the staff could pad the wheelchair or give her an ice pack before he was transferred to Children's for emergency surgery. I shook my head recalling the violence of the birth. She and Ethan were physically bound so closely together, they had to be torn asunder. Who wouldn't want some alone time after that? But I had gotten it completely wrong. What Janet really wanted was to be restored to that primal condition before the birth, where they were still one being. Though I would never experience the elemental closeness of mother and child that Janet felt, I started to understand the depth of their connection. The love I felt for him while sitting together in that chair six weeks ago was perhaps as close as a man could get to feeling like a mother.

I received a message that the prescriptions were ready. Traffic was light, but we had to stop briefly at a construction site south of Bryn Mawr Avenue, while a giant dredger was moved. As I threaded my way around some barricades, Ethan craned his neck to look down into the large hole in the street, where only the tops of the workmen's hard hats were visible. I saw the owner of the Edgewater Lounge wave at me from the opposite corner.

"Save us a table," I yelled out the window.

I should have added "for the day after tomorrow" because it would be a couple of days before the antibiotics and steroids got Ethan up and running again. The bacterial infection plaguing his lungs would clear up not long after. For quite a while, though, he would have a barky cough caused by his flimsy airways rattling in his mostly vain attempt to dislodge secretions from the lining of his bronchial tubes. The croup-like cough, which would continue long after he was fully recovered, could really clear a room. I wasn't offended parents and caregivers shuffled their kids out of Ethan's path when they heard it. How could they possibly know that Ethan posed no infection risk? They were right to be cautious.

He and I would go off the grid until it cleared up, as we had done many times before. Avoiding playgrounds, museums, the library, and anywhere kids congregated, we would spend even more time than we already did at neighborhood haunts like the Old St. Andrews, where we had an especially great family care plan in place. Ethan would configure his train set on a big wooden table with a good view of the El platform. I would signal the bartender when Janet got off the train. A nice cosmo appeared before her as she sat down.

Everyone was so welcoming. At Paula's chocolate ball shop, his term for the True Nature Foods, Ethan "helped" do inventory when he wasn't greeting customers. And we could always rely on the quaint old fire station and many auto repair shops dotting the landscape. Despite their rough exteriors, the firefighters and mechanics rivalled Mr. Rogers in terms of their kindness and attentiveness toward children. On many occasions, they had eagerly explained their work to Ethan and demonstrated how different machines operated. They also let him climb on things, push buttons, and pull levers, much like he would at a children's museum. All of these everyday working people were the unsung heroes of the neighborhood for me.

We pulled to a stop behind a line of cars on a busy stretch of Granville. Two motorists haggled over a parking spot. Other drivers honked and put their heads out their windows to scream at them. I chuckled thinking I would have welcomed such a tussle at times over the last year and a half. Home alone together for days during long recoveries, I was so desperate for adult interaction, I dove for the phone to talk to telemarketers and drew out conversations with Jehovah's Witnesses until they backed away warily, holding their magazines to their chests like protective shields.

I really knew I was at the breaking point one day while watching an episode of Mr. Rogers with Ethan in my lap. Tears welled up in my eyes when Mr. Rogers said, "You make it a special day by just being you, because there's no one else quite like you."

Deeply touched, I had responded, "Thank you, Mr. Rogers," with Ethan nodding his approval.

We finally worked our way around the feud and pulled into the pharmacy parking lot. "Hey, Ethan, let's watch more Mr. Rogers when we get home?"

"Sure. I love Mr. Rogers."

"Me too," I said as we walked into the store holding hands. "Me too."

10 Please, No Thank You, Please!

I PULLED UP MY collar up against the chill breeze off the lake. In such a hurry to get to my favorite breakfast place, I hadn't dried my hair after swimming at the local health club. I dodged people racing in and out of the Granville El station and saw the "Standee's" sign over the sidewalk. The little lightbulbs flashing around the edges warmed my heart. I felt like it was telegraphing a message just for me: "Welcome Home, Jeff!"

Ken tipped his cowboy hat as we squeezed past one another in the vestibule.

"Where's your driver?" the busser, Juan, asked while I hung up my coat.

"I gave him the day off," I responded as I sat down in the booth by the windows. Betty, a waitress with a beehive hairdo and a southern accent, brought me a cup of coffee.

"Let me know when they are coming, and I'll make a chocolate malt for little Harry Potter," she said.

I scribbled in my notebook. So much had happened in the previous week, I was anxious to get it all down before Janet and Ethan arrived. Ten days before, Ethan and I were in the Lakeview neighborhood after shopping for a party that evening. He played on a sidewalk outside a busy café on Clark Street while I trailed behind him sipping coffee and holding a half-eaten cookie. Weaving his way through some bike racks, he paused to say hello to a middle-aged woman. When he began climbing a no-parking sign that leaned heavily to one side, she turned to me and said, "I saw him from the restaurant and noticed how joyful he was running, jumping, and climbing."

"Ethan is a happy little guy. We are very grateful for that."

Both of us watched him hopping from one crack in the sidewalk to the next and back again. Then I asked if she had children of her own.

"I had a son," she answered, "but he passed away some years ago."

That was an answer I did not expect. Overcome with sadness, I said how sorry I was. I wanted to say more, something comforting or wise, but I couldn't think of anything.

"It's been a long time," she said. "It's not as bad now."

She looked at Ethan, who had stopped playing and stood at my side. There was a long pause. We all stood there, warmed by the sun on a chilly day in early December.

Four-year-old Ethan broke the silence, touching her on the hand and asking, "Do you miss him?"

"Oh, yes, Ethan, I miss him very much," she said, coming down on one knee so that she was eye to eye with him. She took a hanky from her purse and dried her eyes.

"What was he like?" he asked.

I looked at him, astonished. *Why didn't I think of that?*

She offered him a gentle smile and rubbed him on each arm before hugging him. Numerous people passed by, looping quickly around us like we were a stalled car. Normally, I would have asked Ethan to move to the side to accommodate them. But I didn't want to intrude.

"I think about him every day," she said. "When I see a lovely little boy like you playing with his mom or dad, I think of all the fun we had together. And sometimes I imagine what he would be like if he were alive today. That makes me happy as well as sad."

Tears welled up in my eyes. Ethan rubbed a tear from her cheek and said, "He still loves you."

She nodded and said, "Thank you, Ethan. I still love him and will never forget him. I feel he is always with me."

"He is," Ethan responded with a little bow of his head.

She kissed him on his forehead. The three of us talked for a while longer, parting after a group hug.

Ethan and I walked silently to the car hand in hand. During the drive home, he ate the rest of his cookie and paged through a catalog of action figures. I glanced at him in the mirror, marveling at his composure and presence of mind. That he knew what to do and say in such a sensitive situation was remarkable for someone his age— apparently even for someone my age too. How could I remain so oblivious to the fragility of life?

Ethan's cardiologist, Dr. Webb, had concluded his last exam by saying, "I am not recommending open heart surgery at this time." She said that every year, and yet I always had the same reaction— stunned disbelief. With frequent pneumonias, surgeries to stretch his esophagus or remove food that had become stuck, and the ever-present possibility of major heart problems, how was I able to continually regenerate a feeling of invincibility? He could die. I should prepare myself for the possibility.

Janet came home early from work that evening to pack the medical supplies for a visit to her parents the next day. Traveling with Ethan was like operating a MASH unit. Humidifier, nebulizer, inhalers, and myriad medications with their own unique delivery systems had to be sorted out and packed in easily accessible containers. Usually, this unenviable task fell on me. I welcomed the break.

We left for the party around six with the goodies we had picked up in Lakeview that morning. The host and hostess, Ruth and Steve, were Ethan's godparents. Ethan and their three kids played together frequently with great enthusiasm and mutual affection. Another family would be there as well. We were close friends with the parents before they had kids, but we had drifted apart over the years. Shortly before we returned to Chicago after two years in London, they had moved down the street from Ruth and Steve. We were looking forward to meeting their children. The youngest boy was approximately Ethan's age.

Unfortunately, it wasn't quite the introduction we had anticipated. Both of their kids were sick, the parents reported. They were feverish and had been vomiting, but they "perked up quite a bit after we gave them some Tylenol."

I was livid. "What's wrong with these people?" I said to Janet in a quiet corner. "The kid is finally healthy, and then this?"

"They just don't understand," she responded.

Kids were walking petri dishes, oozing fluids 80 percent of the time. A minor cold for most kids didn't slow them down a bit, nor did it mean much of a change for the parents or caregivers. For Ethan, though, a minor cold could easily result in a serious pneumonia. I was in no mood to be understanding.

"Either we leave or they leave," I said, ready to explode. "That's it! What other choice do we have?"

"Neither," she said. "There is nothing we can do. The last thing we want to do is offend Ruth and Steve."

We held our breath the entire evening. For once, I wished the kids had not been willing to share toys. But, alas, they were all cooperative little angels, standing cheek by jowl, joyously fingering the same trucks and play kitchenware.

We said our goodbyes and finally exhaled as we walked to the car. "Perhaps there would be a miracle," Janet said. I nodded, still fuming.

That evening we considered postponing our visit to Janet's parents for a day or so to be near his doctors in case he took a turn for the worse. We decided to take our chances and make the trip.

In the middle of the night the following day, Ethan developed a fever. Soon, he was coughing, his entire body shaking with each cough in a vain attempt to clear secretions from his papery airways. Janet held him upright in a chair in hopes of preventing aspiration of stomach acid. His gray pallor and wheezing, however, suggested that significant damage had already been done.

I set to work organizing our supplies. We had everything save his inhaler with the medication that helped clear secretions from his airways. *How could that be?* I frantically searched for it, my hands moving back and forth much like Sylvester searching for the mouse he'd brought into the house the previous year. Ethan's fever and coughing had already rekindled my simmering anger toward our erstwhile friends. About to erupt, I locked eyes with Janet, who was holding Ethan. She looked so sad and worried. My anger abated.

Two hours later, a replacement inhaler from the local pharmacy in hand, I notified the pulmonary resident on call at Children's and hurriedly packed the car. We pulled out of the driveway shortly before dawn.

Six hours later, we were in the ER. Janet and the attending pulmonologist, Dr. Nevin, went over Ethan's medical history while I watched his rapid, shallow inhales with growing concern. *Crucifixion overworked the diaphragm exactly like this.*

I felt a tap on my forearm. Dr. Nevin said, "Don't worry. You're in the right place."

I was in complete agreement. Umpteen pneumonias over the past three years were like being stuck in an amusement park riding roller coasters. The only relief from terror were the brief periods walking from one ride to the next. The pulmonology staff was right there with us the entire time. Their reassuring air of confidence made us feel safe and gave us hope that one day we would finally walk out of the park into a life free of fear.

Janet held Ethan while Dr. Nevin called up Ethan's chest X-ray on a computer monitor attached to the wall.

"This very dark patch," she said, "indicates an aspiration-based pneumonia. These are much harder to treat. He will need to be hospitalized. See the way his sides are pinching in so much when he inhales? These retractions indicate the muscles of his diaphragm are working especially hard to fill his lungs. Giving him additional oxygen through a conventional face mask might not be sufficient to relieve the muscles of his diaphragm. It might be necessary to put him on a . . . that more actively brings oxygen into his lungs."

I couldn't remember the name of this device. She definitely did not say a ventilator. I knew that even then. It didn't matter. The word "ventilator" reverberated through my head and prompted me to blurt out, "You need to put him on a ventilator?"

Janet explained we were concerned about the possibility of additional hearing loss. The doctors reassured us the device was not a ventilator. However, they wanted to avoid more invasive treatments, if they were not necessary, so they proposed inserting a needle directly into an artery in order to get an accurate reading of his blood gases to determine whether a conventional face mask was sufficient.

"By all means, do it," we said in unison.

The nurse gave Ethan a happy pill to relax him. I wished they had given us one. We were both wide-eyed when we saw the needle they would stick up his artery. Feelings of dread may have made the needle seem longer than it actually was, but it appeared to be more than half the length of his little forearm.

The doctors were going to call a nurse to help hold him while they inserted the needle, while we waited outside.

"If it's only a matter of holding his arm," I said, "perhaps you should let me do it." They agreed it might be comforting to him to have one of us there. Janet exited more quickly than I thought humanly possible.

I was startled when I saw the needle as the doctor pivoted toward Ethan, even though I had already seen it. Holding down his wrist with one hand and his elbow with the other, I apologized to him, but I don't think he heard me. As the doctor began to insert it into his artery, Ethan said over and over, "No thank you, no thank you, no thank you." Then in desperation, he cried out, "Please, no thank you, please!"

Janet came back into the room, and Ethan settled down very quickly, offering his mom a gentle smile while she stroked his arm. The doctors returned after a few minutes to say that the more invasive respiratory treatment would not be necessary.

Several days in the pediatric intensive care unit (PICU) were followed by a few more on the pulmonary floor. At first, Ethan sat upright in bed, his chin resting on his chest, his eyes opening only to take medication or receive a treatment. His color gradually improved, and his breathing became much less labored. Awake much of the day, we watched TV together, played games, and did some puzzles.

I was relieved he was recovering so nicely. But the hospital grind was taking a toll on me. Fifteen-plus hours a day at his bedside darkened my mood. I stared at his oxygen saturation levels on the vital signs monitor in hopes of nudging them up enough to gain a discharge. Who knew how long my gaze remained focused on the screen. Eye strain, sore feet, and stiff neck, no matter, I continued peering.

Once again, I felt a tap on my forearm. This time it was Dr. McColley, the other attending pulmonologist. With a smile, she told me all my worry would not cause Ethan's numbers to improve. Only recovery would, and that would come soon. I got the sense I was not the first parent who had attempted to use their unproven telekinetic powers on the vital signs monitor.

After another day in the hospital with no end in sight, Ruth visited and offered to sit with Ethan. Marching around the neighborhood for an hour lifted my spirits. When I reentered the hospital, I felt testy again. I knew I should avoid the pulmonary staff, so that I would not be tempted to badger them about being discharged. *Bam,* there they were at the nurses' station. I nodded as I hurried toward Ethan's room, stopping when I heard Dr. McColley call from behind.
"Do you think your son's ready to go home?"

I stumbled a bit to one side as I faced her, sputtering. "I certainly am certain."

"I think he is as well," she said.

Euphoric, I hustled into the room with a big smile. "Wow, wow, wow," I said to Ethan as I approached his bed.

He looked at me suspiciously and said, "No thank you, please."

Ruth and I laughed. Ethan gave us a quizzical look and continued reconfiguring a Transformer toy.

I thanked everyone at the nurses' station. Ethan gave them a faint smile and a little wave. Once downstairs, we played in the lobby for a minute. Ethan's legs were still a little weak from seven days in bed.

Stumbling around like a drunken sailor, he used his limited energy to play with the kids' displays. It was kind of like he'd been shot several times and yet was still determined to complete his mission. If it's a kid's job to have fun, as it was often said, then Ethan took his work very seriously. It was great to have him back on duty.

"The big boss is here," Betty said as she poured me more coffee. I set my pen down and surveyed my busy surroundings. I'd been so immersed in recording that memory that I had forgotten I was in Standee's waiting for Janet and Ethan. The hospital now seemed a world away, even though Ethan had only been discharged the day before. Several customers laughed and pointed as Ethan opened the car door of his Cozy Coupe with his left hand and swung his legs out like he was getting out of an old roadster. I was delighted he wore the Harry Potter glasses Betty had given him. After waving at everyone, Ethan climbed up onto the seat next to me, followed by Janet. Betty tapped Janet on the shoulder and smiled at Ethan while she placed a chocolate shake in front of him.

"Thank you," he said, before he took a sip. We watched him make a big dent in the shake and cough a bit as he swallowed. Suddenly he pointed out to the street, beaming as a fire engine rumbled by.

I said to Janet, "I'm glad everything's back to normal . . . for now." She nodded and snuggled up next to Ethan.

11 The Feet of Dorian Gray

FROM THE VESTIBULE OF Roosevelt University, I watched people scurry in all directions to escape the early spring downpour. I hurried to my car across Wabash Avenue. A train rumbled by on the El tracks as I opened the trunk and did a quick inventory: chocolate bars with almonds, pretzels, cans of fizzy water, bottles of ready-to-drink coffee, a CD of Virgil's *Aeneid,* and a bottle of wine with a twist-off cap. I chuckled thinking Jake and Elwood had only a half pack of cigarettes for their fateful road trip in *The Blues Brothers.*

The wine bottle fit snugly in a side compartment of the trunk once I removed an empty can of mosquito repellent, three golf balls, and a Phillips screwdriver. Setting everything else within easy reach on the front seat, I sighed about the poor visibility even in the brightly lit parking lot. "At least Jake and Elwood had sunglasses," I muttered, feeling uneasy about the four-hour drive to Detroit.

An electric whirring sound in the trunk forced me to stop at the parking lot exit. Digging through my suitcase for the offending electric toothbrush, I recalled how annoyed I'd been that the US Peace Corps thought Charcot-Marie-Tooth disease (CMT) was a dental disorder. Ready to depart for French-speaking West Africa, I'd received a letter withdrawing my appointment due to inadequate dental facilities in the area. They remained unpersuaded when I informed them CMT was a condition affecting my lower legs, discovered, ironically, by three French doctors named Charcot, Marie, and Tooth.

"Why even put it on your application," my mom had suggested at the time, "since it doesn't affect you very much?"

Okay, Mom, I thought as I shut off the toothbrush and returned to the front seat, *then why did you have me wear clunky metal braces on my legs as a teenager?*

Now, waiting for the light at Michigan and Congress Avenues, I relived the embarrassment of showing up at junior high one day wearing braces attached to ugly leather shoes. Friends said they were not that noticeable. Still, I tried to conceal them the best I could by wearing pants that extended down to my heels. All I could think about as I walked around the school or sat in class were my braces and if they showed. The world was suddenly divided into two classes of people, those with leg braces and those without them. The former was a class of one, while the other comprised the rest of the world, which seemed better off than me just by the fact that they didn't wear braces.

Patches of ice formed on the windshield. I adjusted the speed of the wiper blades and turned up the heat on the defroster. Freezing rain was forecast for the entire trip to Detroit. Two hundred and eighty miles, at night, was a road trip from hell. I had no choice. The new CMT clinic at Wayne State University only saw patients on Thursdays at 8:00 a.m., and I taught Wednesday evenings until 9:30 p.m.

The light changed, but I had to wait for a pedestrian hustling across the street. A car coming from the other direction skidded to a stop in front of him. He slipped and regained his balance by assuming the position of a surfer to the applause of bystanders. *If only I had that guy's luck.*

Moving again, I grimaced as I recalled my mom announcing to my siblings and me that she had to talk to us about something "serious." Shifting back and forth nervously in the uncomfortable dining room chairs, we eyed one another suspiciously, ready to hurl charges and countercharges.

"My father has a condition, Charcot-Marie-Tooth disease, that causes the muscles in his legs to degenerate."

I looked out the window as she spoke, longing to do anything other than have a serious talk with my mom.

"Each of you has a one-out-of-two chance of contracting the condition through me," she continued, "though we won't know if you have it until you reach puberty. That's when the symptoms become evident."

As though I needed another reason to hate my parents at age twelve.

I had no idea how my siblings took the news. I was filled with dread, certain I would inherit it. Sure, there was only a one-out-of-two chance. But an unlikely series of maladies and accidents had already convinced me I had bad luck. A dog scratched my eyelid, splitting it in two; I received a three-inch gash on my leg, cause unknown; I broke both of my ankles while playing on a backyard swing; and I was hit by a car out in front of our house, somehow escaping injury.

These bizarre mishaps, however, paled in comparison to one at age ten. I was involved in a simple game of tag with a couple of kids at a friend's house—up and down the stairs, around corners, and over chairs and tables. I reached my hand out to tap someone's shoulder just as he ran through a doorway and slammed the door behind him. Running full steam into the closed door, my left hand crashed through one of the windowpanes. I pulled it back instinctively, lacerating my hand and wrist.

The three of us rushed into the bathroom and shoved toilet paper into the huge gashes on my wrist and hand. Everything was becoming fuzzy. It was like someone had wrapped thin gauze over my eyes. My friends' mouths were moving, and yet I couldn't understand what they were saying. I slumped to the floor, holding my arm across one thigh. Suddenly, someone appeared in the bathroom. It was a student nurse who was renting a room in the attic. Normally, she was gone the entire day, but she had forgotten a notebook and returned to pick it up. She wrapped my arm in towels and drove me to the emergency room, saving my life.

The major blood vessels in my wrist had been completely severed. I had lost a lot of blood and was in shock. Though the doctors were able to reconnect the blood vessels, the big challenge was the nerves and tendons. People with such injuries in 1968 typically did not regain full use of their hand. Fortunately, a pediatric neurosurgeon from the East Coast was visiting Omaha to give a lecture. He agreed to try a new procedure on me that he had developed for reattaching nerves and tendons. The surgery was a complete success.

My family and friends said over and over how lucky I was to be alive and to have full use of my hand. They were no doubt right. But it was too late. Nothing could shake my belief that I had only bad luck.

Flashing lights from a police car interrupted my self-pity fest. I slowed down to avoid a tow truck hauling a compact car, now a sub-compact car after an accident, away from the entrance to Columbus Avenue. Speeding past a sign for the University of Chicago reminded me of meeting Janet twenty years before. After getting a degree in history from Carleton College, she came to the U. of C. to study library science. The woman simply loved information, craved it, really. The image of her working through the Sunday paper on the porch swing before Ethan got up, brimming with excitement, reporting her findings, made me smile. The Elysian Fields, in her mind, had daily newspaper deliveries and a library open 24/7.

Clearly, the cosmos guided me to her. We were polar opposites in terms of being informed. I knew next to nothing about CMT, a condition that dominated my life. She'd been all over it from early on in our relationship, joined a support group, and followed developments in diagnosis and treatment.

I had boundless energy for exercising, shopping for shoes, and bemoaning my misfortune. Yet not a moment for learning about new treatments, breakthroughs in testing, understanding causes. It even took a twenty-something shoe salesman to get me out of the metal braces. "You know," he said, "they have plastic ones now that might be a lot better for you?"

No, I did not know. But why didn't I? Okay, I was only twenty then. I'll cut myself some slack. And it was 1978, so there was no internet I could surf for information on CMT. I would have had to make a special trip to the library to research the condition. Too busy working, exercising, and partying for that. But eight years later, a graduate student at a renowned research university, countless hours in the library, in seminars, intense discussions with friends. Why not a little bit of time investigating CMT? The fact was such a thought was too unsettling at the time. I had found outlets for my ever-surging mental and physical energy. History, law, philosophy all offered raging streams that would carry me along indefinitely. Flowing with a current kept me from being overwhelmed by anxiety. The possibility of maybe learning something that might have helped me in some unspecified way at a future point was all too iffy then to get me to even glance left or right, let alone leave the torrent carrying me along.

I zoomed past the Museum of Science and Industry and headed south. I continued recalling the chance occurrence that got me out of braces altogether. The plastic braces the young shoe salesman suggested fit so snuggly around my calves, they killed off the hair on the back of my legs and produced painful sores from metal rivets rubbing against my skin. But they also enabled me to increase my already high activity level.

In the winter, I could wear them with boots, allowing me to take long hikes through thick snow, something I never could have done in the metal braces. Plus, with pressure distributed across my entire foot, not just the balls of my feet, I was able to ride my bike much farther and faster. I quickly added so much more muscle to my calves that skin bunched up over the top of the brace, causing another painful pressure point. While I was rushing to a seminar one morning, one of the plastic braces shattered.

Needing a new prescription to get a replacement pair, I made an appointment with a neurologist at the university hospital. I was led into an examination room and sat down next to a cabinet with tongue depressors, cotton, and other medical supplies in small glass containers. A young physician took a seat across from me. *He can't be more than thirty.* Of course, I was often mistaken for a high school student. Like me, he probably also looked young for his age. I concluded he was probably around forty.

After reviewing my chart, he examined my hands and feet, then he had me stand up and hold my balance with my eyes closed, try to walk on my heels, and rise up on my toes. He glanced at the chart again and leaned his head back with raised eyebrows.

"Clinically," he said, "it's not clear you even have CMT, at least not a severe case."

My mind wandered while he went over my symptoms. I was called back to attention when I heard him say, "The weakness in your feet might also be due to the residual effects of encephalitis."

He suggested an electromyogram (EMG) to test nerve conduction, perhaps identifying the cause for the weakness in my legs. Tiny needles were inserted into various parts of my leg muscles, while wires led from the needles to a little machine on a cart nearby. Electrical impulses sent into my legs made me flinch, sometimes mildly and sometimes violently depending on the level of nerve conduction. When the test was completed, he led me back into the examination room and spent a couple of minutes reviewing the printout from the test.

"There is a slight slowness in neural response," he said. "This is consistent with a very mild case of CMT, or it may be a result of encephalitis. It's hard to know for sure which is responsible. It might also be something else entirely. We just don't know."

I glanced at my watch, worried I would not be able to make it to the pool before lap swimming ended.

"Nonetheless," he continued, "it's not clear you should even be wearing braces."

I peered at him wide-eyed and sat forward in my chair.

"The braces," he explained, "hold your feet in place. That's a good thing. For example, it might help deter bone deformities caused by muscle weakness. However, by artificially holding your feet in place, the braces can cause additional muscle weakness. It's like having a cast on your legs; take off the cast and your muscles are atrophied at first because they have been doing less work."

I was stunned. My mind raced while he proposed that I participate in a study about CMT. I nodded while he explained the study, but my mind was elsewhere. It was like an out-of-body experience; images of wearing braces in all sorts of circumstances went through my mind like a movie montage on fast-forward until I exploded.

"You mean, I probably should never have been wearing braces at all? Was this all some sort of mistake?"

I wish I had been more composed. This doctor wasn't responsible for me living more than half of my life in physical discomfort and emotional distress. And what possible good could come from such a reaction? I thought about how different my life might have been without braces. The anger welled up and could not be contained.

He sat upright in his chair, then nervously opened my file. After a brief pause that no doubt felt much longer than it was, he said, "Try to go without the braces for a while. It might be difficult at first because your lower legs are so weak. Eventually, though, you should regain your strength. You will probably always have some trouble with your feet. You do have high arches, for example. But you should be able to get by without braces, particularly while you are so young."

"Boy, howdy!" I called out, with my arms raised in a victory V. I felt as though I had just learned that I'd been pardoned after being falsely imprisoned for life. *Will there be reporters outside?*

"Hard to believe that was twenty years ago," I said to the windshield, which remained, as always, unresponsive. Waiting for the light at Stony Island Avenue, I shook my head about my response the following year, when Janet presented me with some materials from a support group she thought might help me manage the condition. "What? You went behind my back?" I was like someone being carried out to sea, angry with well-meaning people helping him back to shore.

I neared the top of the Chicago Skyway. There was a jolt and kerplunk at each crease in the pavement of the massive structure, which spanned a large industrial zone. Huge cranes, tall smokestacks, and giant slag piles covered in plastic anchored by car tires filled the landscape. A little disappointed to be on level ground again without much of a view, I turned my attention to the audiobook droning on in the background. It was the section of the *Aeneid* describing the horrific punishments in the underworld.

"If Virgil had known my foot care regimen," I said out loud, "he would have included it." It was all so tedious and time-consuming and expensive and tiresome, I wanted to scream much of the time. When I wasn't lubricating and medicating my feet or exercising to keep them strong and flexible, I was being fitted for new orthotics that required considerable experimentation in footwear. Around and around. The big winners in all this were shoe stores. Buying a new pair every three and a half weeks, I was the Imelda Marcos of ugly shoes. Salesmen converged on me like the FBI on a dangerous fugitive when I walked in the door.

Approaching the exit for I-94, I fumbled for coins for the tollbooth. Once through the gate, I put my right foot on the dashboard to relieve a cramp. *Thank God for cruise control.*

My mind returned to my odyssey with CMT. Janet had learned about new blood tests for some forms of CMT after Ethan was born, but she didn't push me to get tested. Who could blame her after my angry response to her support group gambit? When Ethan became unsteady on his feet at times between ages three and four, we wanted to rule out the possibility he had inherited CMT from me.

When I received the letter from the testing company, I hesitated to open it, turning it over a number of times in my hand. Finally, I carefully tore the seal and peeked inside before removing the letter very slowly like it was a potential explosive device. After a deep breath, I read the first line. There it was as plain as day, CMT1. I gasped. "Oh my God," I said to one of our cats, who scampered off to the basement. "I have type 1."

Wanting to be with understanding, sympathetic people to digest the news properly, I dashed to Cunneen's Pub on Devon Avenue. Sitting on a converted church pew, I took a sip of beer, pulled the letter out of my shoulder bag, and read the results again: CMT1X.

"Wait," I muttered. *How did I miss that? X. It is an X-based trait.* Ethan could not have inherited the condition from me. I smiled broadly and slapped the table loudly with both hands, causing the regulars to look over at me. I waved at them with a smile, and they turned back toward the TV.

I watched a little boy approximately Ethan's age amble down the street with his mom. He jumped over a crack with both feet, landing with his arms in the air like a gymnast doing a dismount. Who cared whether or not Ethan would be a gymnast one day. At least he would not have any trouble making his way down the street like my mom and grandfather.

The boy and his mom disappeared from view. I took another sip of beer and returned my attention to the letter. Ethan could not have inherited CMT. But I had the condition, and not type 2. It was type 1, the severe form. A new set of worries crept in. Would I experience a precipitous decline in my condition? Was my right leg worse than the left because of the residual effects of encephalitis? If not, was the right leg a harbinger of things to come?

A loud rumbling startled me. I had swerved on some ice and was driving partly on the shoulder. I quickly got back onto the road. The sight of several trucks and cars in the ditch prompted me to reconsider driving with my leg on the dashboard. Putting my foot firmly on the floor, I focused on driving for as long as I could. After a few minutes, though, my mind drifted back to my hate-hate relationship with CMT.

I recalled how after the initial diagnosis, I watched my maternal grandfather George anxiously, thinking he was a glimpse into my future. His feet turned downward severely and toward the inside. Each step required considerable effort. He often paused while walking to catch his balance. He had thin ankles and little muscle in his calves. This accounted for how much less mobile he was than my other grandparents. My maternal grandmother Che Che still played golf regularly, and my dad's mother, Kate, did most of her errands on foot. Grandpa Joe was famous for knowing where you could get the coldest beer in town. He never owned a car and walked everywhere, easily traversing his hilly neighborhood in Omaha by foot until the day he died. I could never imagine George doing that. At every stage of his life, he must have had greatly diminished capacity.

The same could be said of my poor mom. In her early fifties, her hammertoes were so bad she had to have them straightened surgically. It was heartbreaking to see her confined to a wheelchair during her recovery, metal pins sticking out of her toes. After the surgery she still walked with considerable hesitation and had trouble keeping her balance.

I believed my future was bleak. The only other person outside my family I had ever met with CMT had given me a glimmer of hope. Home on spring break at age twenty-five, I played in a neighborhood platform tennis tournament in ordinary tennis shoes. After my match, I stretched for a few minutes, then eased my legs into the plastic braces. A tall, handsome man, casually though fashionably dressed, asked if he could speak to me for a moment.

"I noticed the braces standing there in a pair of shoes."

"I guess they looked like an invisible man with bad feet was taking in a few minutes of the match."

He smiled, then continued, "When I saw that they belonged to you, I felt compelled to speak to you. I hope you don't mind."

"Not at all," I answered, tightening the straps around the front of my upper calves.

"I was amazed that you could run and jump and twist so ferociously for so long, then strap those braces on," he said, placing one hand on the railing to steady himself. "I have a degenerative condition, Charcot-Marie-Tooth disease. Have you heard of it?"

"Oh, yeah," I responded, nodding emphatically. "I believe I have that too. Hence the braces."

He shifted back and forth on his feet. "I have a very severe case. I've had innumerable surgeries to correct problems with my feet and ankles. I fall down all the time and even have trouble walking."

As he sat down on a bench, I cast a covert glance at his legs, disappointed that his long pants prevented me from getting a good look at them.

"I could never do anything like you just did on the court there. But I have also never worn braces. I see someone at a special clinic at the University of Iowa. You should speak with him. They might suggest something other than braces."

He walked away with a horsey gait. His foot angled sharply down with each step, and he had to deliberately place it squarely on the ground before taking another step. It took him quite a while to disappear around the corner.

After he left, I couldn't remember his name or that of the doctor he recommended. Normally, I would have written it in my notebook, but I was flummoxed meeting someone outside my family with CMT. It was like being a member of a secret cell of extraterrestrials. You may look like everyone else, but you're not really like them. Somewhere, there are others like you. But it is only after many years that you finally meet one. It had really thrown me for a loop.

I finally pulled into the hotel parking lot in Detroit, relieved to have arrived safely in the freezing rain. Out of the corner of my eye I saw an immense pile of trash in the passenger seat. I had randomly tossed candy wrappers, empty bottles of premade coffee, and pretzel bags aside like used ammunition in a desperate firefight.

It was 2:30 a.m. local time. Exhausted but too wired to go to sleep right away, I poured myself a glass of wine and reviewed my materials for the following day. Refreshing my wine glass, I watched a little TV sitting in the big comfy chair in the corner. Waking up there around four o'clock, I plopped on the bed, rolled myself up in the comforter like a huge pig in a blanket, and fell asleep again immediately.

My wake-up call came at 6:30 a.m. With a Midwestern-sized cup of coffee, I hopped in the hotel shuttle to the Wayne State University Hospital. Hurrying across the campus, I imagined being greeted at the clinic by a throng of fellow CMT sufferers exchanging stories and shoe tips.

I sighed when I entered the empty waiting area. After twenty minutes, I was led into an examination room by a young resident, who went over my medical history, tested my reflexes, and conducted an EMG. While she measured my calves, ankles, and forearms, another doctor took a seat to her left and silently looked over some medical charts. After the resident left, he introduced himself as Dr. Shy. We talked for several minutes about my mother and grandfather, and he looked up from his chart when I told him about my encephalitis.

"How did you contract it?" he asked with raised eyebrows.

"It occurred after I had a bad case of mumps as a four-year-old," I responded.

A nurse opened the door and called him into the hallway. While they looked over a chart together, I recalled the only thing that I remembered about having the mumps. Home sick, bored, I had seen a TV commercial showing a group of Boy Scouts cooking fish on an open fire. Determined to emulate them, I built a little teepee with sticks from our yard on one of the gas burners of the kitchen stove. A pan at the ready with bologna in lieu of fish, I turned on the burner and started a raging fire, which quickly spread to the rest of the kitchen. My mother pulled me from the flames and consoled herself with the thought of a new kitchen. A firefighter, worried about catching the mumps, had lectured me about fire safety through the crack in the door of the neighbor's sunporch.

Dr. Shy returned and asked if I had any medical records from that time. "I would be especially interested in knowing whether you had any EMGs done," he said with genuine excitement, before we broke for lunch.

After walking around the area for over an hour, I was disappointed again to return to an empty waiting room. I decided to suspend my CMT outreach program long enough to get some much-needed sleep. After moving a potted plant to get my back flush against the wall, I took a ten-minute nap before being led to a different examination room.

"We've seen many cases of CMT over the last few years," Dr. Shy said, "but your case is the strangest case of CMTX we have ever seen. Your form of CMT," he explained, "varies considerably in terms of severity, but the variance is typically between men and women. Because it is an X-based trait, women tend to have milder symptoms than men because they have two X chromosomes. They might not even display symptoms. In terms of your neural response, muscle mass, and muscle tone, you appear to have a very mild case of type 2. In a male, this is rather surprising. By age sixty, men with CMTX typically require a cane and AFOs to walk."

"What's an AFO?"

"That's short for ankle-foot orthotics."

I explained about breaking out of the plastic leg braces in my twenties because my calf muscles had gotten so big from vigorous exercise.

"I can imagine," he said. "Your calves look great."

I raised my eyebrows, surprised anyone would say that about my partially hairless calves.

"Some time ago," I said, "I'd spoken to a neurologist, who told me that in some cases people plateau, experiencing limited decline. Then, they experience a precipitous decline much later. Am I merely waiting for the other foot to drop, so to speak?" I asked, secretly pleased with my play on words.

"I don't think so," he answered. "CMT is slowly progressive, so your condition will worsen. But you've established a certain trajectory. Your degeneration should continue along the line already established. Your case is interesting in another respect," he continued. "To understand how unusual it is, let me go over some of the most important aspects of your type of CMT."

My mind went elsewhere. It was like a waking dream moving back in time. First, I was speaking with the neurologist at the University of Chicago; then, I was speaking with the mysterious stranger, followed by the shoe salesman—all of whom gave a new direction to my life. Sensing that this moment was important as well, I worked hard to concentrate on what he was saying, yet I was unable to resist the gravitational pull of the past. It was like listening to someone speaking on a phone line with a lot of static. Only individual words and partial phrases came through clearly: "Axox—wire . . . a little bit slowed . . . insulation, myelin . . . slowed conduction . . . velocity . . . axon . . . may explain asymmetries and encephalitis."

This last phrase had caught my attention. Suddenly, there was no static. "Your case is better than most CMTX cases," I heard him say. "There is less atrophy. Why is unclear."

"That's a lot to take in," I said, glancing at my notes, which looked like an experimental poem. Content to let Janet, family science officer, sort out the technical details, I focused on my new principal worry, the difference between my right and left sides. "If my left leg, the good leg, not the right, is the lead indicator of the degeneration produced by CMT, then I feel I'm in good shape. Is that your sense as well?"

"Perhaps," he said. "We will have to study your case more. It may not be possible to determine that conclusively. The fact that you've had encephalitis and CMTX, though, is highly interesting. Your form of CMT involves a protein, Connexin 32. It is a little different from other proteins affected by CMT in that it is located in both the central and peripheral nervous systems. It is in a little different location in each. But there is a possible connection with encephalitis. In a very small number of cases, some activity like high-altitude climbing or deep-sea diving can produce a metabolic shock, which, in turn, might cause a temporary central nervous system problem, in your case perhaps encephalitis, with some of the symptoms you've had."

I was stunned. "Whoa," I said. "What are the chances of that?"

"Not high. There might be ten or twelve known cases of this happening."

I shook my head in disbelief.

He asked, "Do you have any other questions?"

I hesitated. There was one question I knew I should ask, but I was worried I would not get the answer I wanted. After a deep breath, I said, "The neurologist I'd seen most recently said that alcohol damages the sheathing around nerve fibers, so I should give it up immediately. I drink a couple glasses of red wine every day," I added, knowing it was often more, rarely less. "One is for my heart health, and the other because I like it so much." The proportion was actually weighted decidedly toward the latter, but I figured he didn't need to know that. "Is it something I should cut out altogether?" I asked, bracing myself to receive the bad news.

"Whatever you are doing, keep it up. It's really working. In fact, you might want to share some of your experiences with the support group, particularly your approach to conditioning. They may benefit from it."

"I'll do that," I said, making a mental note to join the support group, then added, "It might be a multivolume work," which prompted him to smile before we parted.

As I waited for the elevator, I was positively giddy. You'd think that I had been told that with a simple change of diet or some easy-to-take medication, all my troubles would be over. I still had to contend with the residual effects of encephalitis and the slow, progressive decline of CMT. But I could manage my condition and would not end up like my mother, my grandfather, or the mysterious stranger. For the first time in over forty years, I felt truly lucky.

12 Summer of Silence

TWO WEEKS BEFORE ETHAN'S fifth birthday, I was knee-deep in vines alongside the garage. He was right around the corner. His squeaking hearing aids gave him away.

"Hey, Ethan, could you please bring me the pruners?" No response, so I upped the volume. "Ettthhhhaaaannnnn!!!" Several dogs began barking.

I twisted sideways to grab the corner of the garage with both hands. Arching my back to pull myself in the opposite direction, I saw him playing in the sandbox. "Ethan, come here please, buddy," I said in a loud voice.

"Sure." He got up and walked toward the house with a sandy ruler in hand.

Damn! He thinks I'm in the house. Yanking my front foot free from the vines while my other foot held fast made a disturbing cracking sound. "Shit!" I screamed. This got his attention.

"Hi, Dad, I thought you were in the house," he said, walking toward me.

"I know," I answered, wincing. Once free from vines, I limped past him and picked the pruners up off the table. "I just wanted you to bring me these," I explained, holding them up as if they were evidence in a crime.

"Sorry," he said.

"It's okay," I responded, feeling anger mixed with shame. "It's not your fault. I just needed your help getting the extra pool out from beside the garage."

"Thanks. We really need the extra pool."

I nodded with a forced smile. His fifth birthday only a couple of weeks away, Ethan handled his hearing loss much better than I did at forty-seven. And I was only responsible for handling his equipment. He had to actually live with it.

Ethan returned to the sandbox. I cut my way to the pool and dragged it to the other side of the yard. Collapsing in a nearby Adirondack chair, I mused about the challenges of managing Ethan's hearing aid technology. Earlier that day, an hour after we visited the audiologist to be fitted for new earmolds, Ethan reported that one of his hearing aids was making a loud crackling noise.

"Like a tire running over glass," he said, with his uncanny ability to describe sounds he probably couldn't hear fully.

I made an appointment for the following day. Loaner hearing aids were generally in short supply. He already had one loaner while his left hearing aid was in the shop. He did surprisingly well with only one hearing aid. Still, it had to be harder for him being shorthanded, so to speak. To complete the technological perfect storm, the FM trainer, a miraculous though temperamental device that transmitted sound directly to his hearing aids via radio frequencies, was also malfunctioning.

He played away in the sandbox. I was delighted that he was so happy and confident despite his daily struggle to understand. Still, he was becoming aware that hearing loss distinguished him from other children. A few weeks before, he asked a question that we had anticipated with dread.

"Mommy, why did God make some children who need hearing aids?"

"Because everyone needs help with something," Janet answered matter-of-factly. "Some people need help seeing," she continued, "so they wear glasses like your dad and me."

"That's why Charlie and I are best friends," he said. "Because I need hearing aids, and he needs glasses."

I got up to clean the pools. Bending over to scrape some caked-on mud off the sides and the bottom, I was grateful he hadn't addressed the question to me. I would not have handled it as well as Janet. "Because life sucks," while true, was not helpful developmentally.

I took my frustration out on the pool, blasting the remaining dirt with the hose. Getting sophisticated technology to function properly was way beyond my capacity. At least I could make dried mud bend to my will.

"Look," Ethan said with a smile, drawing my attention to the sandbox. "I rebuilt the tower." I gave him a thumbs-up while I pondered whether I wanted to hobble over to turn the hose off. The pain in my ankle persuaded me to remove the nozzle with the water running instead. Water shot in all directions as I loosened the head from the hose, giving me a welcome drenching. The sun sparkled in the water, and I thought dreamily of pulling off my clothes and lying in the pool for a while with my nose barely above the waterline.

Waiting for the pool to fill, I moved an Adirondack chair next to the sandbox and watched Ethan work. "This is going to be a lot of fun tonight, favorite guy," I said when he smiled.

"Yeah, thanks for doing the party."

He scurried off to find squirt guns while I dozed off in the chair.

Waking to the sound of hard plastic landing at my feet, I surveyed our arsenal—mostly small arms, and only a few of the big blasters the kids like so much. It was probably for the best. They cause a lot of collateral damage. Even sitting comfortably on the deck like royalty far from the fray, the adults might still get soaked. We definitely wanted to avoid an impromptu middle-aged wet T-shirt contest.

I turned my attention back to the pools. Watching the water level rise slowly in the second one, I became lost in thought. The summer was rapidly drawing to a close. Ethan would enter full-day preschool in less than two weeks. The consensus view among stay-at-home parents was this was a cause for celebration, as they would finally have more time to themselves. There was certainly a lot I wanted to do. Swimming during the day rather than at five in the morning would be a nice change, as would working on projects in sunshine, not in the garage under a trouble light. And I'd have time in the stacks at the University of Chicago Library, like in the old days, following my muse wherever it led. At the same time, though, I knew I would be a little lonely with him in school all day. I really enjoyed the free-flowing days with him. Days off from school wouldn't be the same. Now, we felt no pressure to seize the day. There was always tomorrow.

Staring down at my feet, I didn't notice Ethan standing next to me. He put his little hand on my shoulder and asked, "Are you okay?"

"Oh, yeah, thanks," I responded. "Hey, buddy, why don't you grab a book? Let's read for a while together."

After he scampered off, I looked down at my troublesome hooves. The new orthotics I'd gotten at the CMT clinic helped a lot. Extending up a couple of inches above my shoes, they enabled me to stand more squarely on my feet, which now did not turn as far outward while I walked. Sometimes there was rubbing on the bony knob, the lateral malleolus, on the outside of my ankles. That was a small price to pay for walking better and becoming fatigued much less easily. My sprained ankle confirmed there was not a lot that could be done for my right paw. Dante's right foot trailed behind him at the beginning of the *Inferno*. Perhaps this meant I, too, would get out of foot pain hell one day.

A half hour later, Ruth and Steve arrived with Jasmine, Sergio, and Rosa. They joined Ethan at the sandbox while the parents settled on the back deck. I took drink orders and returned quickly with libations.

"This is hilarious," Ruth said, when I handed her a drink. "You have turned your deck into a bar."

She was right. I had, though unintentionally at first. I had rebuilt the deck after two-year-old Ethan gave us a real scare when he found his way onto a railing over an eight-foot drop to hard concrete. In addition to making it kid-safe, I added shelves atop the railings for food and drinks, a cabinet with serving trays, and a few decorative touches typical of pubs in the UK. A neon martini sign was on order.

The other guests, Jim and Holly with their kids, Charlie and Henry, arrived just before Janet. The adults stood along the front railing to watch the kids. The Ott kids were in the pool, while Charlie joined Ethan and Henry at the sandbox. Ethan hurried off to start the water and ran back, finding a spot next to the other boys, who knelt with piles of toy boats and potential canal locks lying at the ready in front of them. There was a good deal of shouting and gesticulating. They began adding boats and locks seemingly at random. The fact that the system seemed to work so well suggested the addition of flotsams and barricades was more systematic than it had appeared to me during the construction phase.

Ethan's voice soared above those of the other boys. His speech therapist, Renee, had said recently that he was having trouble monitoring the sound of his own voice. Between the ill-fitting ear-molds and malfunctioning hearing aids, he couldn't tell that he was speaking much more loudly than the other kids. His voice had taken on a slight metallic sound over the summer. I missed the timbre and the beautiful melodic quality of his speech from before the extended hearing aid crisis.

Slide races commenced. Ethan and I had consulted earlier about how to configure everything, and it was all working as planned. The pools were set alongside one another. We angled the two slides in such that the kids came into the water close to one another without actually coming into contact. This gave them the feeling of danger without really putting them at risk. Hitting the water simultaneously produced a tidal wave–like splash. Anyone standing along the edge of the pool felt the full force of the wave hit their midsection, forcing them back a step. Part of the wave shot upward to their chin, causing them to laugh and shake their arms from side to side. The remaining portions of the wave splashed out to the sides, with trace amounts landing on the boys in the sandbox.

"Well, Jeff Seitzer," Ruth said, emphasis strongly on the word "well," "the Seitzer household is clearly the temple of kid fun."

"I'm glad," I responded with a smile. "I wanted to end the summer with a bang."

"Well, congratulations," she answered. "You succeeded."

A squirt gun fight broke out, and the kids ran in all directions exchanging fire. The pools became the kid equivalent of the watering hole during a drought featured routinely in nature shows. Everyone had to return to one for more water, but this exposed them to danger, not in the form of a crocodile waiting in the shallow water for easy prey, though, just a barrage of fire from kids who had already reloaded. Shifting alliances formed. Boys against girls, older kids against younger kids, the Ott family against the Crilly family with Ethan first with one family, then another. Occasionally, a stray stream of water reached the deck, prompting Ruth to call out, "I felt that," followed by laughter and further conversation.

After a few minutes, I went inside to fill drink orders and encountered Ethan and Charlie in the downstairs bathroom filling up water balloons. Water was already all over the sink and the floor.

"What's going on, guys?" I asked, already knowing the answer.

"We're going to throw these off the upstairs deck," Charlie reported. I waited for the inevitable follow-up question.

"Can you tie the water balloons for us, Jeff?"

"Of course," I responded, "but you guys need to agree to something."

"Sure," Ethan said, beaming at his partner in crime. Charlie handed me a water balloon to tie and one to Ethan to hold.

"First and foremost, no leaning over the side. And be sure that you don't drop any on the adults. That will bring an end to things very quickly."

They both nodded, though I was certain they were too excited to process anything I'd said. Ethan, not wearing his hearing aids, probably heard little of it. Charlie lost his grip on one of the water balloons, sending a powerful stream of water directly into his face. I gave him some paper towels, then continued with a raised voice, "If any adult asks you to stop, you must stop. And you will have to take a turn below being bombarded as well. Agreed?" I said, looking them both directly in the eyes.

The entire exchange was for my benefit, really. Not very comfortable as an authority figure, I would rather have been throwing the water balloons from the upper deck onto my peers. I had to maintain a semblance of order, for the kids' sake, at least.

Outside, chaos reigned. The dogs of war had been released. The adults stood along the railing, sipping drinks and chatting, while the kids exchanged squirt gun fire and heaved water balloons at each other. The renowned military strategist Carl von Clausewitz argued that the great challenge for military commanders was to transcend the natural limits of the scale of conflict. This was in the nineteenth century, of course, before the advent of incredibly destructive weaponry. In the twentieth century, the challenge became limiting the scale of conflict. It wasn't so hard in our case. The last water balloon met its end on the stone path. That was my cue to intervene.

When I reached the railing of the upstairs deck, I took two squirt gun shots to the face. "Thanks a lot," I said as I held my arms up to signal a cease-fire. "Okay, kids, everyone hold your fire. Have a little more to eat. Then, we will do the rocket balloons."

The kids jumped up and down as though Santa's sleigh had landed in the backyard, full of presents four months early. "Rocket balloons, rocket balloons!" they chanted loudly. I waved to them as though they were cheering for me.

Steve and Jim volunteered to manage the launch. The kids assembled on the upstairs deck and cheered loudly when they stepped out. They jockeyed for position with some minor squabbles before the first balloon fell harmlessly to the ground, prompting grumbling among the kids and a sigh from the adults.

The next rocket balloon streaked away from the deck, glanced off a tree limb, and skirted along the very top of the neighbor's garage roof, before disappearing into the alley.

"I didn't think about what would happen if they were successful," I said as another wafted into the neighbor's backyard. Their dog Sparky chased it around, jumping and biting at it, keeping the balloon aloft.

It, too, disappeared in the alley over the low-lying chain-link fence after weaving its way through the garden with Sparky's help.

Several rocket balloons went straight over our garage into the alley, while the last one wound itself around the defunct cable line crossing the backyard diagonally. The kids left the upstairs deck and appeared on the back porch for a debriefing. They talked over one another recounting the notable successes and failures and drifted down into the backyard. Ethan and Henry surveyed the badly damaged canal system while the rest of the kids looked for squirt guns. Before a new fight could break out, Janet and Holly pressed their way into the middle of the pack and organized a search-and-rescue mission for the expended rocket balloons.

Dessert was ready when they returned. The kids arrayed themselves throughout the backyard, a few on the big stump in back, a couple at the table near the grill. Ethan sat alone on a small stump by the sandbox. The adults talked while I watched Ethan. He seemed a little withdrawn, no doubt a little tired. Who wouldn't be after a day like this? But he had the added challenge of having to work so much harder to understand what was being said.

Ethan walked up to Rosa and said something to her that I couldn't hear. With bowls in hand, they walked together into the house. After a while, I checked on them. They sat on the basement floor wearing my biking gloves, Ethan the right one and Rosa its companion, while they played the Honey Bee game.

I recalled a picnic in Millennium Park earlier in the summer. Ethan and Rosa had held hands as we walked to the lawn. Ethan only had one hearing aid functioning then. But they clearly knew each other so well it didn't matter. He walked along the edge of the walkway, one foot on the curb while the other was on the sidewalk below. Without speaking, they switched back and forth, one spinning around the other's back to take up the position along the curb. I was touched then by the fluidity of their movements and how they silently initiated and executed the switch as though responding to an internal signal.

He had been among his people that day. Malfunctioning hearing aids did not matter so much. It would be an uphill struggle for him once school started, though, if his hearing aids weren't working properly. Resolving to get them in order by then, I went back upstairs and rejoined the party.

13 The Petite Man's Guide to Parenting

ETHAN AND MISSY, BOTH now five, chased each other around the large sculpture adjacent to Pratt Avenue Beach. With only inches separating them, they ran through the large loop in the center, then around the low-lying section on the north. I marveled at how the space between them remained remarkably constant, as though they were connected telepathically. After crawling through a small opening, they fell on top of each other, laughing and rolling side to side.

They were both easy on the eyes. Ethan was tall and slim, fair-skinned with a thick mop of hair, wavy and dishwater blond, while Missy was willowy with a beautiful light-brown complexion and curly, dark-brown hair. Their eyes were round and sparkly, Ethan's blue and Missy's hazel.

I was so caught up in watching them play, I had not noticed that a dog had ambled up to me until it licked my ear. Watching it run off to its owner, my gaze fell on the apartment building on the other side of the traffic circle where Missy and her mom Babette lived. What a great spot! A three-story brick structure with perhaps twenty-four units, all with Juliet balconies offering great views of the lake. I hoped that the gentrification wave spreading through the North Side of Chicago would stop short of this neighborhood, where yoga teachers like Babette could still afford to live.

She came through the gate and crossed the traffic circle. A former dancer, she moved effortlessly across the rough pavement and uneven terrain. We chatted about what the kids had done and exclaimed in unison about how beautiful the lake was before she told me that she had just received a request to sub a class at the East Bank Club and wondered if Missy could hang out with us until she got back.

"Of course," I responded, adding with a wink, "Don't forget, instructors are supposed to use the side door there, not the front entrance."

She smiled before scooting over to talk with the kids. I was relieved things had cleared up with Babette. Six months ago, Ethan and Missy had their first playdate together outside the kids' gym at our health club. After I had dropped Missy off, Babette and I chatted about summer camps.

She blurted out, "My husband was a petite man like you. I prefer petite men because I can beat them off, if I have to." I stared in stunned silence as she turned to talk with the kids, as though she had merely shared news about a new household product. My mind raced to figure out what I might have done to offend her. I snapped to attention when she looked back at me with a calm expression, thanked me for hosting Missy, and said that we should do this again the following week.

Afterward, I walked Ethan to a nearby playground. While Ethan and another boy climbed, jumped, and slid their way around the jungle gym, I called Janet, my training supervisor, for a debriefing.

It was the summer of 2005. The Iraqis were drafting a new constitution at the time. I chuckled thinking that a PhD in political science had better prepared me to predict the draft constitution's prospects for quelling sectarian strife in that war-torn land than it did the actions of parents and caregivers. After five years as a stay-at-home dad, I had made some progress in grasping their complex emotional makeup. Janet was instrumental in that. When I was taken aback by things people did and said, Janet explained the likely reasons for their behavior and suggested how I might respond to it.

My on-the-job training began in earnest when Ethan had play-dates beginning around age three. These were mundane affairs, with the mom and I making polite conversation while the kids played excitedly at our feet. We always parted on good terms, often agreeing on a date at the other house. When the agreed-upon day came, some moms were a little skittish and evasive. Avoiding eye contact with me, they'd speak to Ethan directly.

"You are welcome when so-and-so's daddy is home," or "We will come over when your mommy is there too." I found it a little comical when they would sometimes add, "Okay?" as though Ethan had any say in the matter.

"It sounds like it's about the dad, not her," Janet had said the first time this happened.

"You mean," I responded with raised eyebrows, prompting her to nod, "if guys did more childcare," I continued, "they'd know that afternoon delight is the last thing on your mind when playing Duck, Duck, Goose or chasing runaway kids into the street. You really just want a shower, alone, and maybe a nap."

She laughed. "I wouldn't make too much of it. I'm sure that possibility wasn't even mentioned. Something like, 'Oh, so Ethan *and* Jeff were over to play in the basement today,' from the dad was probably enough to make the mom anxious about how he might react if you were over again. In the future, try to find play opportunities that don't involve you being alone with the mom."

Since it had always been the dads who complicated things before, I was a bit surprised when Babette, a single mom, was apprehensive about me. I viewed Janet as a tarot card reader for her seemingly uncanny ability to understand social situations that I found baffling.

"You and I had always spoken with her together," Janet explained. "That was the first time the two of you were alone."

"Yeah, except for Missy and Ethan and innumerable park visitors," I responded.

"Nonetheless," she said, "Babette's probably used to guys coming on to her. The fact that she was so calm and didn't press the issue further suggested that you had not done or said anything inappropriate. I think it was a shot across the bow," she concluded, "meant to warn you not to intrude on her personal space."

"Like the Bush administration's doctrine of preemptive self-defense in Iraq?"

"Hmm . . . maybe. Anyway, follow her lead. Next time, just pretend like nothing is out of the ordinary. I am sure it will be okay."

That day's playdate extension confirmed it was okay. With an entire afternoon ahead of us, Ethan, Missy, and I drove to Andersonville. First my monthly purchase at Alamo Shoes, where they each got a helium balloon, followed by the toy store next door. Balloons placed under my care, the two of them worked their way through the inventory to pick out something they could do together at lunch.

Outside again, balloon custody transferred to them until excitement about petting a cute dog loosened their grip enough to send the balloons on their way to Cleveland. We hurried across the street to Charlie's Ale House, bumping into Ethan's preschool teacher, Joan, at the entrance. We talked about the happy hour/playdate Janet and I had hosted two Fridays before. The entire preschool—all four classes, parents, kids, siblings, caregivers—was there. There were kids in the basement, in the attic, in the back and front yards, all through the house, everywhere. It was like a play vortex.

"I still can't get over the flyer," Joan said with a hearty laugh. "'Cocktails for the parents/cookies for the kids.' You were wise to put cocktails first," she added. "It probably got more parents there."

"Sorry it raised kind of a fuss at school," I responded, referring to a complaint someone had lodged with the principal about the cocktails reference. "It is a Catholic school after all," I said in my defense. "That's what sold Janet the Methodist on the parish, serving alcohol at church events."

"Me too, by the way," she said with a smile. "I wouldn't worry about it. It was a great thing for everybody."

Settling into a cozy booth, I recalled Joan and her kids making a surprise visit while Ethan was in the hospital. Ethan had made so many great friends in the first two weeks of school, Joan explained. The kids really missed him, so they'd made a book of pictures and messages to remember them.

The waitress arrived with menus and some crayons. Ethan and Missy played tic-tac-toe on the placemats until the waitress returned to take our order. When she left, they read a comic book together. Their chirping about the drawings reminded me of Ethan's ongoing commentary as he paged slowly through the book his school chums put together. Joan understood the precariousness of Ethan's life—not only that his health could deteriorate fast but also that his illnesses separated him from other kids. Two weeks for kids Ethan's age was like a lifetime. To help him stay connected, she had suggested I bring him to circle time and recess until he was ready to return full-time. It had worked like a charm. His first day back was like he had never been gone.

Waiting for our food, Ethan and Missy made bracelets while I sipped my beer. Jewelry-making was probably not Ethan's first choice of things to do. Still, he was happy to go along. What mattered to him was establishing an enthusiastic connection.

Each of us wore sparkly new bracelets by the time our food arrived.

"Oh, Ethan," Missy said, giggling, as he made origami figures from his french fries. He smiled and asked if she wanted to draw something together while they ate.

Afterward, we stopped at the Salvation Army on Bryn Mawr Avenue to inventory the toy aisle. Ethan and Missy were exclaiming over a large doll with a retractable tummy and removable organs when I noticed someone waving at me from outside the window. It was a mom from the neighborhood whose son was a friend of Ethan's. Setting up playdates with her was a bit complicated because of what I had come to call her six phases of the moon.

She was always very friendly and exuberant in the first encounter, the exact opposite in the next. In the subsequent four encounters she became progressively friendlier until the cycle began again. That day she was in the friendliest part of her cycle. A full moon. I had to set up something right then, or it could be another month before I had another chance. I met her at the door, where we agreed on a date the following week.

Walking north on Clark Street, the neighborhood became less glitzy. Most of the businesses had a distinctly old Chicago feel: liquor stores selling Old Style and Budweiser, not fine wine and craft beers, *panaderías* without gluten-free items, and beauty salons with obsolete hair dryers. I liked to browse the shops along this stretch with Ethan because the businesses were more kid-friendly than many of those in the more gentrified areas to the south. On this side of the line, the owners' kids were often in the shops and in a playful mood.

In a clothing store for kids' dresses and suits, Missy held a frilly number up to a full-length mirror while Ethan and the owner's daughter nodded their approval. I ambled around with their excited chatter in the background. Looking through a display of kiddie cummerbunds, I felt a tug on my arm. It was Ethan, who whispered that he wanted to get a stuffed animal for Missy.

As they walked up the street side by side, Missy clutched her new pink bunny. She deliberately bumped into him to get his attention, then said, "This is a date," with a big smile.

Ethan denied it, though not too vigorously, as we walked slowly to the car.

We lingered at a drop-off bin for clothing donations. They took turns opening the hatch while the other made voices of someone inside.

"Let me out!"

"Sneakers, please."

"Come back later; I'm busy."

We left when Babette texted to say she was on her way home. After I rang her bell, I watched the kids walk along atop the retaining wall ringing the courtyard, chuckling about how naive I still was. Because Ethan and his friends were now old enough to be at one house or the other without a chaperone, I didn't think there would be any more cause for concern. *Wrong!* I was astonished to learn some of the moms thought I was hitting on them when I asked to set up a time for their child to come over after school.

"Don't they realize I'm looking for a playmate for Ethan, not me?" I asked our friend Megan, who had told me this.

"Give them time," Megan had responded. "They are used to guys who are only friendly when, you know, they are on the make. It will be okay once they get to know you."

Ethan and his friends were eager for more time together. I

volunteered often in the classroom and had trouble not granting their requests for playdates. So, I decided to change tactics. Instead of approaching individual moms, I invited everyone to the all-preschool happy hour/playdate Joan and I had discussed earlier. Both the moms and dads of Ethan's school chums met Janet and got a glimpse into our home life, easing some of their concerns about me. Setting up playdates was much easier afterward.

I also gained valuable intelligence on the parents. Like a scientist observing animals in their natural habitat, I was able to identify their good and bad qualities, how they behaved toward other parents, how they interacted with their own kids, and whether they cared at all about other kids. This helped me decide whether and/or how to approach them about getting our kids together individually once their apprehensions about me had been eased.

Babette arrived. There was a nice breeze off the lake while she and I discussed getting the kids together again the following week.

While walking to the car together, Ethan said, "Thanks for inviting Missy. We always have a good time together."

I nodded with a smile and opened the door for him. Climbing in myself, I recalled something a tactless mom had said to Janet at the all-preschool happy hour/playdate: "So, you really do exist," as though the whole stay-at-home dad thing was just a ruse on my part.

"And I thought I was clueless," I muttered.

Driving down the street, I realized I viewed each family as an independent country with its own history and distinctive culture. Piecing together their formative influences and charting their patterns of behavior was engaging. But it also made me more effective at my unpaid internship facilitating Ethan's evolving friendships. I now approached the frequent pleas from other kids to play with Ethan like requests for closer diplomatic relations. To gain approval from the family government, I had to discern the contours of their unique comfort zone and develop a workable strategy for maneuvering us into it. Then, the kids could do their jobs of developing a relationship without fear of an interruption of diplomatic relations.

At the stoplight, I glanced at Ethan, who was busy removing and replacing organs in the doll with the retractable tummy we had bought at the Salvation Army.

Maybe being a political scientist was not bad training for being a stay-at-home dad after all.

Well, that is, if you were lucky enough to have a librarian on retainer.

14 Here's to Friends!

ETHAN AND I STOOD inside the unfinished playhouse on a warm summer morning. The sky darkened while we discussed the design of a cabinet with sections for him and for his baby sister, who was slated to arrive soon from China. A thunderclap drew our attention to the yard, where the wind wreaked havoc. A plastic covering blew off a table and deposited plates, glasses, and a candle in a line ending just before the stone path. The covering continued its flight across the yard until it became draped across the opening of the rose arbor. When a plastic kiddie pool came tumbling toward us, we dashed off to the front porch.

Rain came down in sheets. We sat with our chairs set flush against the house and enjoyed the feeling of the cool spray on our bare legs. Sylvester came around the corner of the porch steps, drenched, and scurried under Ethan's chair.

After the rain tapered off, we stood at the top of the porch steps. There was a gentle tapping sound in the foliage and gutters above us. Ethan's eyes moved from the leaves to the gutters, suggesting he heard it as well. Without his hearing aids, he might not hear what were for me some of nature's most enchanting melodies—waking up from a deep sleep to the sound of rain pattering against the window or birds chirping on the sill. Perhaps seized by the same thought, Ethan handed me his hearing aids and said, "Tell me when the rain stops."

He hopped from puddle to puddle down the sidewalk until he bumped into Sean and his mom, Karen, who waved before walking back down the block. The boys leapfrogged between puddles in one direction and kicked their way through them on the way back before running inside.

They came down from Ethan's room both wearing Calvin and Hobbes shirts. Dropping their wet things in a big pile on the living room floor, they scurried down to the basement barefoot. I followed closely behind with their soggy castoffs pressed into a big ball against my chest. Halfway down the stairs, one of the shoes squirmed out and tumbled down the rest of the way after careening off the side wall. I started over at the bottom, dropping everything into a big pile and picking it up again.

As I rounded the corner, Ethan said, "Remember last year we had the piñata, and my parents forgot to put candy in it? We banged it over and over again, and it was in pieces, but—"

I started the dryer hoping the noise would drown out their rehashing of that particular parental misstep and hurried past them while they were bent over in laughter. Sean's response reached me when I was halfway up the stairs.

"That was so funny. Next time you should fill the piñata with Legos."

Why don't they just fill those things for you? Probably some food safety regulation with demonstrable health benefits. But I liked Sean's idea about Legos. *Surely there's no reason they couldn't do that?*

A half hour later, they rumbled through the kitchen toward the backyard, one of Ethan's hearing aids dangling from the top of his ear. He displayed no pain when he deftly pushed it back in place before exiting.

A few weeks before, an angry cyst had formed near the top of that ear. We thought it was from his hearing aids rubbing against his skin. The nebulizer face mask had produced a similar welt on his face when he was a toddler, which went away on its own after lubricating the edge of the face mask and taking antibiotics for a year. After we tried warm compresses on this one for a few days without results, a friend pointed out that its proximity to his brain was a concern, so off we went to the ER.

There we learned that it was another birth defect related to TEF/EA—a pouch that often occurs at that spot in children born with a coarctation of the aorta. Looking back, we realized there had always been a dimple there, which we considered a nice distinguishing mark. We weren't upset about the doctors not telling us about this possibility. Sometimes the pouch becomes infected, we learned in the ER, and must be removed, sometimes not, so why trouble us with it until a problem develops? We certainly were not wanting for further worries.

Another thing they didn't tell us ahead of time was that they might have to shave some of Ethan's hair during the surgery to remove the cyst. The prospect of another surgery did not faze Ethan, but it would have been a different story had he known that he might have his head shorn. I had learned not long before how attached he was to his magnificent mane of thick, wavy, wheat-colored hair.

On a whim, we had stopped in for a quick trim at a new salon in the neighborhood. I assumed it would be uneventful. I should have been on my guard, though, after the stylist told me while cutting my hair that she did not see her grandkids out of fear that she would be heartbroken if they moved away one day. Things went south when the "iron grandmother" cut Ethan's hair.

Responding to my entreaties to stop, she said, "*Your* hair, it is too beautiful to cut short. It should be long." She lopped off several inches of Ethan's hair. "*His* should be shorter."

Standing helpless at her side, I wondered if she was as imperial with her own grandkids' hair. If so, she had good reason to fear they might move away.

I shuddered recalling Grandpa George's barbershop terrorism. Getting out of school, excited about walking home with friends, perhaps going off to play somewhere for a while . . . surprise! George would be leaning against the door of his big Chrysler. *Zzzzz, zzzzz.* Buzz cuts. His chums laughed as I protested and flinched when the clippers nicked my ears. Moving away from family, friends, and the familiar surroundings would have been a small price to pay to avoid those torture sessions.

I felt like I had really let Ethan down. There wasn't much I could have done apart from physically restraining her. Still, I had gotten him into this situation and was not able to stop her. He didn't seem angry with me, but I wouldn't have blamed him if he had been. Hair style is a deeply personal thing. The guys at our usual place, Father and Sons, where Ethan got his very first haircut, understood this. The iron grandmother gave him no say in how he wanted his hair cut that day. Anyone would be upset.

Walking home, teary-eyed, Ethan bemoaned the loss of his "friends." Perhaps he liked his hair long because they made his hearing aids less noticeable. If so, it didn't seem due to the sort of self-consciousness I'd experienced while wearing leg braces as a teenager. As far as I could tell, his self-image wasn't adversely affected, as mine was. It was the endless questions about his hearing aids that he found tiresome. That was why he reluctantly agreed to have the teacher say a few words about them at the beginning of his first year at his school.

He had better things to do than explain over and over why he needed to wear them.

His hair had finally grown back shortly before the cyst formed. When he came out of surgery, his hair had been slicked back, and at first we were afraid it had been cut on one side. What a relief it was when the junior surgeon, Dr. Silverman, pulled us aside and whispered that Dr. Holinger had wanted to shave Ethan's head, but that he persuaded him to spare Ethan's "friends" by using some gel to hold his hair back. That was a big ask. A few years before, Dr. Holinger had told us that he had cut hair in college. We had shared a laugh about his disappointment in not being allowed to redeploy those long-dormant skills.

Now on the back deck with a cup of coffee, I listened to Ethan and Sean's excited chatter about a construction project they were envisioning. Ethan's pronunciation, enunciation, and vocabulary were all excellent. Any parent would be pleased. I certainly was proud of him. He spoke with such excellent pronunciation and with such an extensive vocabulary despite severe hearing loss. The lad could really turn a phrase, not only in everyday conversation but also in the poems and short stories he had written. I was also relieved that he was speaking at all.

Since the initial diagnosis, the possibility of additional hearing loss hung over our heads like a sword of Damocles. The thought that he might slide into a world of silence prompted us to take sign language lessons in addition to having him in speech therapy. Now, not quite three months before his eighth birthday, we were able to breathe a bit easier. His language skills were so well developed that even if some calamity caused further hearing loss, he would probably continue to speak well.

Ethan and Sean stood nose to nose, going over the details of their design. I enjoyed listening to them complete one another's sentences, the last few words said in unison, as though the lines were rehearsed. They were soul mates, inseparable since they met two years before. Nothing had come between them until a classmate made Sean pinky swear that he would only play with him at recess, not Ethan. I was outraged and offered to intervene on his behalf. Ethan explained that Sean did not want to hurt the boy's feelings, and he did not want to put pressure on Sean.

"Don't worry," he said. "Sean will come back to me," and he did.

I found it remarkable that even at that tender age he understood that relationships ebbed and flowed, with periods of great excitement followed by those of relative calm. *And* he was happy to back away when things weren't clicking and reengage when the energy returned. He felt none of the angst that prompted his classmate to try sealing him off from Sean.

That was a kid desperate to survive socially. I had to give him a break. It was some of the parents that really got me. One day at the playground when Ethan was four, I overheard someone say to another parent that she did not allow her son to play with Ethan because he was deaf and would hinder her child's language development. Concerned about losing my temper, I scooted over to the other side of the playground like a prizefighter returning to his side of the ring after the bell. She deserved a stern lecture. However, I had to stay on good terms even with parents I found objectionable. The deck was already stacked against Ethan. Hearing loss, eating challenges, pneumonias, and me as his handler made him a bit of an outsider. I didn't want to add to his troubles by giving people yet another reason to exclude him.

Fuming in my corner of the ring, I asked myself how her attitude differed from other forms of discrimination like racism. To paraphrase Dr. Martin Luther King, someone should not be judged on the basis of whether they wear hearing aids but rather by the content of their character. Ethan might not have heard everything, but he didn't miss a thing, particularly on how to be a good friend. That mom should have included kindness, imagination, understanding, and humor, not just hearing ability, into her screening process for her kid's friends. Having Ethan as a friend might have helped her child's moral development, or perhaps better yet, hers.

The sound of metal scraping against concrete drew my attention back to Ethan and Sean. They were dragging a large metal tub out from under the deck. Each of them gripped a handle with both hands. They picked it up and walked sideways with it across the yard. With a thump, they dropped it in front of a statue of the Virgin Mary, whose head was turned down and to the side. It appeared as though she were examining the new addition to whatever project they had going. *Perhaps she had some ideas she wanted to share with the architects?*

Listening to Sean and Ethan discuss their plans for the tub, I marveled at how flawlessly they both spoke for their age. I thought back to the mom evaluating her kid's friends with an eye to her child's development. That was a parent's duty, one might say. I wondered, though, about her child's language abilities now. Were they comparable to Ethan's, the borderline deaf kid, whose speaking ability and writing skills were exceptional by any measure?

Ethan's ability to connect with others softened my anger. Children with hearing loss sometimes struggled socially, although Ethan had not, despite all the obstacles he faced. He would find his way socially regardless of parental narrow-mindedness. In fact, his hearing loss might have contributed to the development of his advanced social skills. On innumerable occasions, he peppered me with questions about various combinations of gestures, facial expressions, and phrases in different contexts, all with the aim of learning to understand people when he could not hear what they said. An astute observer of people and of social situations, he was able to find something in common with almost everyone and figure out a way to make the most of it under varying circumstances.

I went to the railing to check on them. Ethan poked his head out from under the deck to ask me to help them get some stuff out of the garage. While I was setting up sawhorses for them, my neighbor Carol called out from her screened-in back porch, "What are they doing, Jeff?"

"Gathering materials for a play structure for some mice they've caught," I answered, not expecting her to take me seriously.

"Ooookay," she said, drawing out each syllable to make clear her disapproval. "Do you really think that's a good idea?"

"Perhaps not with Sylvester outside," I responded. "Thanks. I'll bring him in."

She shook her head and turned the volume up on her TV.

Inside making sandwiches, I thought about other parents micromanaging their children's friendships. I was probably the dopey one trying to bring kids together because they had a good rapport, not because I wanted to be friends with the parents nor because I imagined the child would contribute to Ethan's development in some way. There were too many unknowns. How can one predict how things would work out? The best approach, it seemed to me, was to experiment and see how things developed.

Heading out with the sandwiches, I recalled Karen telling me Sean was quiet after she and his dad split up, but that he'd started to talk again after Ethan came over to play regularly. Sean also had a positive impact on Ethan, bringing out his creative side. They were good for each other because they had fun together. I was glad Karen was also willing to let their relationship flower.

I put the sandwiches on the table and went inside the playhouse to finish framing the roof. Serious construction delays made me feel a bit under the gun, though I wasn't completely at fault. Most recently, it was because skylights were added to the original design after Ethan informed me it was to be "more of an artist's hideout than a playhouse." An artist needs light, after all, we concluded in a status meeting held in the sandbox. But enough is enough, he must have been thinking the week before when I showed him the plans, for he had said, "So far, you have built *zero* artist hideouts."

After about a half hour, Ethan and Sean shrieked with delight when they had completed their contraption. I popped over for a quick inspection. It started with a long piece of discarded gutter posed atop the back of an Adirondack chair. There was a gradual descent toward the back of another chair. The sawhorse also had a gutter balancing across it. *That's clever.* But that wasn't the most remarkable feature. One of the plastic reticulated rainspouts was wound through the opening at the top of some garden fencing so that the wide end was positioned upward to catch whatever fell from the second gutter. The narrow end was wedged through the opposite side of the round fence. It was attached to the second piece of reticulated rainspout that angled down across a milk crate, ending above a large tub of water. *Maybe that use of the tub was the Virgin Mary's idea?*

Standing shoulder to shoulder at the end of the track, they put a toy car on the gutter and ran alongside while it sped around the track. Everything worked perfectly. The gutter across the sawhorse functioned like a teeter-totter, dropping the car into the bendable pipe. It then slalomed around the second pipe into the water, making a muffled thud at the bottom.

The two of them jumped for joy. I congratulated them, gathered up the remains of the sandwiches, and headed inside. Carol stopped me at the top of the stairs.

"They decided against using the mice?" she asked.

"Yeah, they put them back under your porch. Should I send Sylvester over?"

She looked at me blankly.

"There never were any mice, Carol. It was a joke."

She laughed and turned back to her TV, while her husband Dave gave me a big thumbs-up. Carol was a good person, very welcoming and hospitable. She just had an exaggerated need for order and too much time on her hands to fret about all the things out of place. It didn't help that she had the Addams Family for next-door neighbors. She was riled up much of the time about many things, and I was usually within earshot. Earlier that week, I had talked her through something truly harrowing: a bicycle locked to a no parking sign across the street "for two whole days!" Dave, who got this all the time, appreciated that I teased her a bit.

Ethan tapped me on the shoulder at the bottom of the stairs and handed me his hearing aids, which were still squeaking. He and Sean had dredged out some squirt guns and started blasting each other from different sides of the obstacle course.

"Be sure not to spray the Andersons," I called out.

"Okay, Dad."

I turned off his hearing aids and put them in a baggie I carried in my pocket for such occasions. After stowing the sandwiches on the deck, I stealthily filled up a squirt gun, inched my way into range, and began squirting the two of them. They wheeled around and began blasting me. My glasses were so covered in water I couldn't see them. I pressed forward anyway, their squeals of delight confirming that I was hitting my mark.

15 Alligator Tales

THE WAITING ROOM WAS packed. Already there two hours, I was troubled by the thought that my body would be permanently misshapen by all the time I had spent sitting on hard plastic chairs. The fleshy part of my rump, pushed up and away from the bony part of my backside for extended periods, might one day not return to its original position. Long after Ethan ever stepped foot in a hospital again, I would be forced to walk around with a bum that jutted out sideways.

I joined Ethan at the perpetual motion machine wedged between the hallway and a row of chairs in the waiting room. It was an elaborate system of twisted, bent wire tracks that conveyed a set of balls around and through a number of obstacles like a dog's head that swung back and forth, sometimes opening, other times blocking, the entrance to a narrow bridge. Near misses at various openings built up tension; varying speeds of the climbs and descents lent a sense of urgency to the slow progress toward the ultimate goal. After a ball finally overcame all the obstacles, a chain carried it slowly to the top, where the whole process began anew. The precision and intricacy of the design, along with the exact timing of the coordinated movements, was astounding.

We were there for a swallow study, a moving X-ray of the so-called simple act of swallowing, which was anything but simple. In fact, it reminded me a lot of the perpetual motion machine in the lobby. Ethan had taken the first such test as a toddler strapped into a little chair. Although they called it "the throne," it did not lessen the appearance of being set up for a firing squad. He had to fast beforehand. Not feeding your toddler, interestingly, was as difficult as trying to feed him. Starving, thirsty, he pointed and lunged toward the liquid sweetened with chocolate and the mac and cheese, all mixed with barium. As they fed him tiny amounts, he would reach out his hand, opening and closing it over and over to signal his desire for more.

For Ethan, now almost eight, the test was routine. Settled on the exam table, he read while the radiologist went over the procedure with me. I struggled to stay focused. It was 11:00 a.m., and we still had a six-hour drive ahead of us. I tried to channel Janet, who would say something like, "Just be patient. She has to go through it all. Let her finish so we can be on our way. It's not that long a drive," etc. etc. I felt the tension welling up inside of me. Up early exercising, followed by packing, I was exhausted and completely on my own. Somewhere, I assured myself, the world's smallest violin was playing for me.

With Ethan's lead lap gown in place and the radiologist and I safely behind a protective wall, she flipped a switch. The elaborate machinery above Ethan produced a very loud hum, as he started drinking the chocolate-flavored barium mixture. We watched the dark liquid career wildly through the complex system of shoots and accelerators that comprised the human throat. I was transfixed, yet again. Umpteen years of higher education, and all I could say was, "Wow!" after each little twitching, twisting movement propelled the dark liquid or food particles farther down his throat.

Once on the elevator, Ethan turned toward me as he pressed the button. Face aglow, his smile was framed by traces of the barium mixture, giving it a slight clown-like look. "I can't believe we are going to Adventureland. Thanks for taking me."

"My pleasure, buddy," I responded, trying to conceal my apprehension.

He danced a little jig while walking down the hall. Bouncing up and down on the seat in the waiting room, he said, "I wish Mom and Penelope could go with us. Don't you?"

"Oh yeah, that would be great," I said, pleased by the thought that Janet and I could trade off doing roller coaster and hearing aid security duty.

After a few minutes, we were in an examination room. Ethan sat on the swivel chair near the desk and began spinning around with a smile on his face. His unruly mop of hair stuck out in all directions. I wondered what an aeronautical engineer would say about the aerodynamic effect of his hair. He very quickly got up to a fast rotation speed. At each pass, he said, "Hi, Dad!"

I tried to time his passes so he was looking at me when I said, "Only one more spin."

He stopped on a dime without my prompting when Dr. Holinger entered and shook my hand. In one step, Ethan sat next to me. Dr. Holinger looked Ethan in the eye and extended his hand.

"How have you been, Ethan?" he asked. "You've grown quite a bit. How old are you now?"

"I'm seven," Ethan responded. "But I will be eight soon."

"Those are both great ages," Dr. Holinger said, prompting Ethan to nod emphatically. "How's your summer been?"

"Fantastic," Ethan answered with a big smile. "You'll never guess where my mom is!"

"Where?"

"In China picking up my baby sister. Her Chinese name is Guo Li," Ethan said very slowly and deliberately. "That will be her middle name. But we will call her Penelope," he said, sounding out each syllable.

"Penelope?" Dr. Holinger said. "That's a beautiful name. Did you pick it?"

"Me, my mom, and my dad. We all did," Ethan answered. "We waited a long time for her to come to us, like Penelope did for Odysseus to return. That's why we chose it. But my mom says that everyone calls her LìLì in China, so we will call her that too."

"Those are wonderful names," Dr. Holinger responded. "Thank you for explaining them all to me. I'm sure she will be worth the wait and that you will be a wonderful big brother." He smiled.

Ethan returned to his book while Dr. Holinger reported that no stricture had developed in his esophagus. This meant that it was not necessary to stretch the surgical site, where as a newborn his esophagus had been detached from his trachea and reattached in its proper position.

"That's great news," I said, rapping my knuckles on the table. "Last time, you said that at Ethan's age, you would do the dilations right here in the office?"

He nodded. I winked at him before I turned toward Ethan, who was so absorbed in his book he had probably not heard us. "Hey, buddy, how about we have Dr. Holinger do a dilation right here before we get on the road?"

"Ah, no," he said with a smile. "Maybe next time."

Ethan returned to his book, while Dr. Holinger explained that Ethan's reflux levels were also good. When he was younger, Ethan had so much reflux that during one shallow study the radiologist ordered his assistant to stop feeding him the barium mixture because his esophagus was already filled with it. The assistant signaled that she had already stopped. Reflux had completely filled his throat. That amount of stomach acid surging up your esophagus routinely meant trouble. Besides irritating and perhaps damaging the delicate esophageal lining, high levels of reflux increased the chances of Ethan aspirating it through the cleft in his larynx.

Packing up our stuff, I glanced over at Ethan, who looked over a detailed anatomical drawing of a throat. *He must have a very high pain threshold.* Heartburn was intensely painful the few times I'd had it, and Ethan must have been experiencing it all the time. From his demeanor and behavior, you never would have known. Not a bit of complaining. Esophageal dilation without anesthesia? Easy peasy.

I couldn't remember the last time Ethan's esophagus was dilated. I took it as a good sign that I couldn't remember exactly. I was also fuzzy on the total number. My best guess was sixteen so far, eleven bunched together in his second year. Janet had said that many TEF children have sixteen dilations in a year, maybe more, year after year. *Things definitely could have been worse.*

At a restaurant across the street, I sipped an iced tea while Ethan ate his hot dog. It was slow going for him. He had to chew a very long time before trying to swallow. I nudged his milk closer to his plate to remind him to take a drink to ease things on their way.

Everything was going down well. No coughing, no choking, nothing stuck. I wondered how much lower my blood pressure would be if I didn't instinctively hold my breath while he was eating. It was hard not to freeze up a bit.

"Sometimes children with Ethan's condition are eating on their own within two years," his speech therapist Kristin had said when he was a baby. "Sometimes, though, they never fully eat on their own and require a feeding tube for their entire lives."

We appreciated her candor. I should say Janet did. I personally kept singing the lyrics to a Sheryl Crow song, "Lie to me, I promise, I'll believe."

Ethan took a big drink of milk between bites. After a few seconds, he looked sideways, the signal that he was preparing to swallow. I still found it miraculous that when he was not yet one year old, Kristin had taught him that by turning his head slightly to one side and twisting his neck a bit in the other direction, he could often shepherd food and liquids past the surgical scar and around the gap in his larynx without major incident. The announcement "mind the gap" as doors opened on the London Underground always went through my mind when Ethan turned his head like that.

Now that he was older and more practiced, he didn't move his head as deliberately when he swallowed. Something like a hot dog with a bun, however, still merited a sideways glance. Even so, swallowing remained a slow process. After weaving its way past the gap, food was now in the esophagus. This phase was smooth sailing for most people, but not for Ethan. Weakness of the muscles lining his throat meant he had to work very hard to squeeze the balls of food into his stomach. Everything moved very slowly, and there were frequent pauses along the way, much like an urban train system operating on lines of track under repair.

As he took another bite, I imagined an educational cartoon. Ethan was a tiny tour guide leading a group of food particles into his stomach. The group tiptoed past his larynx like they were walking along a slender ledge atop a deep chasm. Then, they slipped through a narrow passageway formed by his surgical scar. Once in the esophagus, he moved behind them and pushed them slowly down the esophagus into his stomach, much like the transit officials in Tokyo pushing people into the crowded subway cars. Every once in a while, he stopped to catch his breath and lubricate the sides of the passageway with some liquids.

Thankfully, food rarely got stuck anymore, and when it did he was able to cough it up without too much difficulty. The choking episodes when he was younger were horrifying more for us than for him. We stood by nervously then, aware there was little we could do to help him besides give him sips of carbonated beverages in hopes that the bubbles would help him clear his throat. He always remained calm, holding his hands up, palms facing the panicky adults to signal that he was okay. And he was always very cheerful once he cleared his throat.

"All done. Ice cream please, Mommy."

I smiled at him now while he carefully chewed his food. Appreciative of the effort eating involved for him, I felt very proud of him at that moment.

He noticed me watching him and asked, "What are you thinking about?"

"Just wondering how Mom and Aunt Joan are doing. They meet Guo Li today. I hope it goes well."

"How could they not love her?"

I was charmed by his optimism. So excited about the prospect of having a sibling, he couldn't imagine life not being better once she was here. Of course, no one could predict how things would turn out. There were simply too many unknowns. Each new addition to a family alters the circumstances and relationships in ways one can't fully anticipate. This would be the case regardless of whether the child was born into the family or adopted into it. Would our quite cozy threesome become an uncomfortable foursome? Perhaps. Having a child always required a leap of faith.

What Janet and I shared was a sense that our family was incomplete.

We had more love to share, so we had to take the chance. For Ethan, though, it was perhaps even more pressing. He was outnumbered. He needed someone on his side, someone all his own. Ethan had oodles of friends and enjoyed time to himself to pursue his myriad interests, reading, painting, music, stories, and cartoons. He wasn't lonely and would have a rich life as an only child. But having someone to shower with love, a sibling with whom he would always be connected, sometimes closely, other times not, but always connected, would make him whole in an ineffable sense. Hence his boundless, unconditional love for someone he had not yet met.

Tummies full, we walked to the car discussing roller coasters. He reaffirmed his decided preference for those that turn upside down.

"Hmm," I responded, "I'll have to get back to you on that. I'm not sure what I think about looping around upside down."

"It's fine, Dad, really. You're strapped in. You'll love it!" he added excitedly as we reached the car.

"What about our stuff? Will it be strapped down too?"

"Yeah, good point. I'm thinking yes."

"Oh, well. I guess we'll find out," I said, worried about what to do with his hearing aids.

We arrived at the hotel in the early evening, giving us plenty of time to splash around in the mini water park the building housed. The pool had a fake rock formation in the middle with several slides in the form of tunnels that emptied out into different sections of the pool. Ethan quickly found his way onto the rock formation and down the slides. I was glad he was enjoying himself. It was all a little nerve-racking for me, though. The pool was full of adults and kids of various ages thrashing about. I was worried he might come down into the pool and be inadvertently pushed underwater by someone frolicking near the slide. The entryways for the slides were alongside one another. Not always sure which one he entered, I might be waiting at the bottom of the wrong slide. After about an hour of trying to guess where he would come out and moving into position to ensure he was okay, hotel officials ordered everyone out of the pool. We waited with other hotel guests along the edge of the pool flush to the wall, pressed a bit too closely together for anyone's comfort. After about twenty minutes, they announced the pool was closed. We learned later that someone had defecated in it.

It was a great disappointment for Ethan. I was content to get off work early that night, though I might have chosen a different means for my deliverance than human sewage in the hotel pool. Still, we had time to unwind properly and get a good night's sleep.

We were the first people in the park the next day. Ethan talked nonstop about what he wanted to do as we hurried toward the roller coasters visible on the horizon. Then, to my surprise, he insisted we visit a section of the park with mostly little kid stuff. The verbal torrent continued, though on a new topic: what his baby sister would like. His portrayal of her reactions, as he imagined them, was so vivid that I started to believe she was padding around with us.

The age difference between them still worried me. When we applied for the adoption, Ethan was halfway through his fourth year. With the typical wait then at six months, we expected they would be three years apart, maybe less. It took over three and a half years for the adoption to be finalized, making Ethan six and a half years older than her. Would they be able to relate to one another? When I was a kid, a one-year age gap hadn't mattered at all in terms of being friends. A two-year difference meant you could be okay friends. Three? Fuhgeddaboudit. And simply because Ethan was so determined to love her didn't mean she would love him in return. Watching him pick out a souvenir for her, I felt anticipatory heartache thinking of the possibility that she might reject him.

We loped along with the nose of a new stuffed animal poking up out of my backpack. Rounding a large cotton candy stand, we encountered our first roller coaster. Ethan ran to get in line, jumping and pointing the entire way. I was quickly at his side.

It was an older wooden version that mostly involved a lot of up and down and around movement, nothing upside down, which was a relief. The line was moving very quickly toward a display with a picture of a little boy and girl with numbers along the side. A height requirement. *I'm saved. He'll be disappointed, of course. But we'll find something to do.* I was crestfallen. Forty-two inches? He was already much taller than that. No restrictions. I grimaced as he enthusiastically reported this fact to me.

Our turn came. We climbed into a little metal compartment with a roll bar and shoulder harnesses. I quickly stowed away his hearing aids and checked to make sure he was securely fastened. Pretty flimsy. *It must work, though*, I told myself, *otherwise it would not be operating . . . or would it?* With a jolt, we were off. Up and down and around we went at varying speeds. At each turn, we were smashed into the wall on one side or the other. Ethan squealed the whole time. I would have preferred a bike ride on a new trail that had opened recently nearby. But after a moment or two, his enthusiasm began to have an effect on me. I was starting to enjoy myself. We were both squealing with delight.

I led the way to the next roller coaster, one with loops where the car was upside down briefly. Earlier in the day, the very thought of careening along upside down was terrifying for me. But here I was, a convert, won over by Ethan's passion for the momentary panic and excitement each ride provided. What a relief it was to fit snuggly in the compartment. The roll bars were also much more padded and fit tightly on our shoulders. When we made our first upside-down loop, we dropped a bit into the padded roll bars. It gave me quite a fright, though Ethan seemed unfazed. At least his expression never changed from pure, unadulterated excitement.

I decided to give up fretting about the safety design of the rides and had a blast doing every scary one in the park with him. They closed the gates behind us when we left.

The pool was open when we returned to the hotel. Though I was a little reluctant to enter the water, I figured I'd survived a day of being suspended upside down, eating doughy pizza, and drinking runny beer; I could withstand a little residual fecal matter.

Before falling asleep, we were lying in bed looking through some photos we had purchased. One was of us in a log ride into a tank of water that splashed all over us. He was beaming, while I was expressionless. "We have a lot of fun together," he said, snuggling up against me.

"We sure do," I answered, a little embarrassed that I was not able to feign a smile in the photo.

"You know, I think it's going to be even more fun with Penelope here."

"Definitely," I responded. "It will be an adjustment, though. You won't always be able to do everything you want."

"I know. But that's okay. I think it will be great to have someone to do stuff with. She would have had a lot of fun today."

"Which roller coaster would she have liked the best?"

"The upside-down one, definitely," he answered. "But we'd secretly have to hold her up for her to pass the height requirement."

"A small price to pay for fun."

He was quiet for a moment before asking, "Do you remember when you did the alligator with me? You would come up the stairs before I went to bed. You banged on each step with your hands. Each time it would be a little louder."

"And you would jump up and hide, calling out, 'Mom, look out! The alligator is coming.'"

He thought for a moment, then asked, "Are you going to do that when Penelope's here?"

"Sure, though I thought maybe I'd have you do it."

"I don't know," he said. "I think you should do it. You are her dad, after all."

"Hmm . . . maybe we could do it together?"

"Great idea. It will be even more fun that way. Good night, Dad," he said, turning over on his side.

I looked at him for a minute before turning out the light. "Yes," I said to myself. "It will definitely be more fun that way."

16 Thank You, Bàba

ETHAN CALLED OUT FROM behind as we rushed up the stairs, "Dad! Dad! Wait, I forgot something in the car."

"It's important, Dad, really," he added once we reached the landing.

The "something" in hand, we caught the train and reached the terminal as the plane landed. Countless travelers, blank-faced, passed through the security barrier near their gate before Ethan suddenly began jumping up and down, pointing. "There they are!"

Janet, Aunt Joan, and LìLì stopped to share a long group hug. LìLì cried when Joan set off in the direction of the parking garage shuttle, waving to us as she disappeared through the exit.

As Janet and LìLì approached us, Ethan plopped down at my feet and began playing with an array of toys. I glanced at him, puzzled. After waiting anxiously over three years for this moment, why was he playing with toys he had clearly aged out of long before? I felt Janet's arm around my waist. She kissed me and put LìLì down. We watched as she toddled up to her new brother, slowly turning herself around and backing her way down onto his lap. They played away in their little cocoon while a stream of harried travelers flowed around them on either side. *Hence the urgency about the "something."*

Walking through the airport, as LìLì clutched Janet and gazed at Ethan, I thought about Janet, the militantly well-informed librarian, so worried by reports that some adopted children have trouble bonding emotionally with their new families. Why all the fuss? Eighteen-month-old LìLì was clearly already bonding with us.

It wasn't long, though, before I realized that the "us" did not include me. The next day, we were hanging out in the backyard. First Janet, then Ethan, went inside the house, leaving me alone with LìLì, who was too busy herding toy farm animals into a barn to notice them leave. After she closed the gate behind the last one, she looked up at me, glanced around for them, and then looked back at me. Her face crumpled. She closed her eyes, pointed at the house, and began to cry.

Such a tiny thing, so fragile, and clearly very unsettled in her new home. Even in China she had bounced around for eighteen months between foster homes, hospitals, and the orphanage. Complete strangers whisked her away, and she must have felt like she was being kidnapped. After a rocky two weeks in a hotel with people who looked and perhaps even smelled different, she'd landed in a place where the climate, vegetation, furniture, toys, and house pets were alien.

Perhaps she would have been more comfortable with me if I had been there in China. We had decided Ethan and I would stay home because we thought that the generally poor air quality in China might be a danger to Ethan's fragile respiratory health. Ironically, that was during the 2008 Beijing Summer Olympics. The Chinese government had instituted closures and restrictions that significantly lowered pollution levels, which meant the air was probably cleaner there than in Chicago.

I had to figure out a way to put her at ease. This was kind of uncharted territory for me. I'd never had trouble connecting with kids before. Married already fourteen years before Ethan was born, we had spent countless hours with the children of family and friends. At gatherings, parties, even chance encounters, offspring of various ages found their way to my side. I had searched for caterpillars, cataloged seashells, read books, engaged in sword fights—both conventional and laser varieties—and acted out little dramas; I played store and dress-up, sometimes even playing store *in* dress-up; you name it, I had done it at some point with practically every youngling in our milieu.

We went around and around for years on the issue of whether to have kids. Janet had many concerns. There was the whole "How could we bring a child into this world?" consideration, which was a cliché for most people save Janet, who did not just believe it. She actually knew a lot of depressing things about the world other people overlooked, some, like me, deliberately. On a more personal level, she fought depression, had low energy, and doubted she would be able to watch her child suffer, as all parents must do at some point.

Seeing her hold babies, practically melting as she pinched their chubby thighs, I knew she would regret not having one of her own, or at least not trying. So, when she said that she would try to get pregnant if I were fully on board with it, I put my finger firmly on the getting pregnant side of the scale. Of course, I'd understood being fully on board differently than she did. I assumed that meant playing with him or her at my convenience, as I had done with all these other kids over the years. Most of the heavy lifting of raising a child would be done by her and professional child managers like day-care providers and teachers. As it turned out, if cluelessness were an Olympic event, I would have been a gold medalist.

Eight years in the trenches with Ethan, as unprepared as I was to be his caregiver, and as difficult as it was at times, produced a very close bond between us. I hoped for a similar feeling of closeness with LìLì. I didn't want to be just a party motivator anymore, winding kids up, then passing them off to their parents. I wanted to be *her* father.

After three months, Janet went back to work, and I took over LìLì's care full-time. Feeding her shifted me from the edge to the center of her radar screen. She always had a voracious appetite, the orphanage had reported. It was hard to keep her fed. In China, her little hand spirited ribs off Janet's plate at adoption group dinners after she had licked her own clean, and her nimble fingers were active at our dinner table as well. Yet she was still seriously underweight. Putting her on a restricted diet, we learned she had trouble digesting dairy, soy, and gluten. With these eliminated from our menu, she grew like a weed. Her appetite, considerable before, increased dramatically. She shoveled everything in with great gusto—ribs, steak, chicken; pears, apples, bananas; broccoli, asparagus, peas; and rice, pasta, beans.

One day, exhausted from near constant food prep, I turned around to find her beaming at me from her high chair. She waved a chicken leg in each hand like a miniature Henry VIII. I had become a player.

We also had considerable cuddle time during her naps. I tried to put her in her crib after she fell asleep while reading together, but she woke up immediately and cried inconsolably with her arms outstretched. It became routine for me to stay in the chair with her. Three to four hours was a long time sitting still for someone as hyperactive as I was. Her tiny head on my chest, breathing in unison, helped me cope with being motionless for hours under a heavy blanket. I was equally antsy holding Ethan for extended periods during his first few years. Yet I knew that it probably contributed to his deep emotional security. Penelope, who came to us at eighteen months, was making up for lost time. I was happy to do my part.

She became steadily more comfortable with me. There were fewer and fewer apprehensive scans of the horizon when she found herself alone with me. She glanced back at the house less frequently when I walked away with her in the stroller. After several weeks, she only had eyes for me, that is, when neither Janet nor Ethan were available. We spent our days reading, coloring, and playing in the basement and the backyard. We went to playgrounds, visited the zoo and the kids' museum, and hung out at coffee shops and the health food store. The two of us had become inseparable companions, as Ethan and I had been at her age.

One day at the playground, I was trying to entice her onto a set of round disks fixed by chains to the top and the bottom, which wobbled as you moved from one to the next. A few older kids watched me demonstrate and began crossing with me. She couldn't resist joining them with my help, all of them squealing in mock terror as I called out that there was hot lava below them. We moved on to the swings, where with each upswing, I ducked under her as she swooped overhead. She laughed, kicked her legs, and patted her hands on the harness. After the umpteenth pass, she called out, "Stop, Bàba!"

She had been calling Ethan "Gēgē" and Janet "Māmā," Chinese for "older brother" and "mom," respectively, for quite a while already. But until then she had used no name for me. Now, when I plucked her from the swing, she placed her hands on my face and pulled me close. Nose to nose, she said, "Xiè xiè, Bàba," Chinese for "Thank you, Daddy." The tension I had been holding inside drained away. I kissed her on the forehead, awash in relief that she had begun to accept me as her father.

A few weeks later, we met our friends Dan and Hesper and their two girls, Olivia and Abbey, for dinner at the Silver Seafood to celebrate LìLì's second birthday. It wasn't your typical Americanized

Chinese restaurant. The mostly Asian clientele spoke what I assumed was Chinese. The huge fish tanks in the back were clearly not decorative. The glass was cloudy, and the fish disappeared through the course of the evening, no doubt becoming part of someone's dinner. Much of the food being carted around was not recognizable to me and was even hard to describe. The most memorable dish looked like a large, deep-fried rib cage, pointy bones sticking up everywhere.

Janet said the post-Cultural-Revolution-style decor reminded her of China. LìLì must have felt the same way. When we walked in the door, she became very quiet. Olivia had brought a book and was willing to read to her. Usually, LìLì was thrilled to have the undivided attention of an older kid. But she did not respond, which was not like her at all.

The food arrived. Standing between our chairs, LìLì kept one hand on Janet's shoulder as she sampled food from each of our plates. Egg rolls from mine, shrimp and ribs from Janet's. Between bites, she glanced at the other tables. After a big spoonful of chicken fried rice, she sidled over to a young Asian man, turning around to catch another glimpse of him as we scooted her away. A few bites later, this time orange chicken, she ambled over to another young Asian man at a different table. She was quiet the rest of the evening. When her silence continued into the next day, it became clear to us: LìLì and her words were on strike.

When she arrived six months before, she spoke only a baby version of her Chinese dialect. Her English vocabulary grew very rapidly until she had become a regular chatterbox, speaking mostly English seasoned with a few Chinese words. Then, she stopped speaking without any apparent physical cause. We worried she was not attaching to us emotionally.

It was the middle of winter then. All spontaneous kid life had stopped. No time at the playground, no chance encounters with other families to break up the monotony. Just the two of us, inside all day, mano a mano, with LìLì making animal sounds and bobbing frantically at things with one arm extended.

After five days, I was at my wits' end. As we sat on the floor together mid-morning, LìLì panted with excitement while turning a toy around in her hands. I braced myself when she dropped it and fixed her gaze on a doll to my left.

"Just say, 'Bàba,' LìLì, and I will bring it to you," I pleaded. Partly, I wanted her to call me "Bàba" again. Worried that we had lost the emotional bond we had formed, I craved reassurance.

I also thought that it might help her feel more at ease. It was wrong to project adult feelings on such a young child. At some deeper, unconscious level, though, LìLì might have still been traumatized about leaving China. I knew myself how difficult it was to speak a foreign language, how fatiguing it was to adapt to another culture, having studied in Germany and England for almost four years. While I had thoroughly enjoyed my time in Europe, I sometimes felt the urge to be myself, reverting to my accustomed ways of speaking and acting even at the risk of offending others. Maybe LìLì was experiencing a two-year-old version of this desire. My hope was that encouraging her to use this linguistic remnant from her time in China might rekindle her desire to speak.

It didn't work. She lunged and reached and grunted with even greater ferocity. I sighed and handed the doll to her while I went back over that evening at the restaurant for a clue about how to get her out of her funk.

The image of her staring at the young Asian men brought to mind something Janet had read in reports about LìLì's foster homes. She was especially close to a foster brother at one of the homes. Perhaps that helped her bond so readily with Ethan. Even more telling, though, was the report of how deeply attached she was to her first foster mother. LìLì was quiet and kept to herself after she arrived at her second foster home. The foster father there, however, made regular excursions to the playground with her, which helped fun-loving LìLì come out of her shell. He came to her aid when she felt vulnerable. Perhaps seeing these young Asian men sparked a memory of her foster father or rekindled residual feelings for him.

LìLì patted the doll's hair and straightened its blouse. I imagined this kind man delighting in her smile and enjoying her enthusiasm up until the moment she left. Among the many losses she had already experienced in her short life, the forced separation from her foster father must have been especially painful.

Though I had never met her Chinese foster father, I was still in awe of him. He knew that she would be with him for only a short time, and yet he risked loving her fully. *He* was her bàba, not me. I realized I had to stop worrying about whether she accepted me as her father and focus instead on having fun together.

Lying on the floor, my arms at my sides, I rolled toward her, as I had done with Ethan many years before. She stood up and laughed as she tumbled over me. Numerous reiterations followed before we faced each other again. She gestured toward the doll. I took a deep breath, then said, "Say, 'Da-Da,' LìLì, and I will give it to you."

She looked up at me and appeared to consider this proposition. Finally, she nodded and said, "Da-Da." I held up the doll, but she walked right past it onto my lap. We read a book while LìLì talked the entire time.

Hearing her speak again was magical. I was mesmerized by the movement of her lips. The sound of her voice filled me with joy.

I was also sad she wouldn't be calling me "Bàba" anymore. It had the charm of the exotic. More importantly, though, it was an ongoing reminder of that magic moment in the park when I thought she had finally accepted me as her father.

Mixed with the sadness, though, was admiration for our little human dynamo's tenacity in holding her ground, and her loyalty to her bàba. Her unconquerable spirit was one of the things we loved most about her. She could call me whatever she wanted. I was simply glad she was comfortable with me again.

I thought about her Chinese foster father while I reached for another book. I did not want to displace her bàba. My gratitude to him precluded that. By loving her selflessly, he had found a place in her heart. Since she had made a space for him there, it gave me hope that one day she would make one for me as well.

17 Grand Central Station

ETHAN AND I STOOD at the back window, watching a bunny work its way through the thick blanket of snow covering the backyard.

"Do you think there will be school today?" he asked.

Giant snowflakes brushed against the glass before being pulled quickly away by some invisible force. The snowfall thickened farther away from the house.

"I doubt it. Are you disappointed?"

"Uh, no," he responded, drawing out each syllable for emphasis while shaking his head.

Public school closures were announced on the radio. That was my cue to begin calling half the parents in Ethan's class, the unenviable task I shared with the other room parent Kristi, whose kids, Jack and Chelsea, were friends of Ethan's.

"Damn!"

"You've got to be kidding!"

"Not again!"

"What am I supposed to do now?"

I didn't take offense. Their reactions were completely understandable since most parents still had to work. Teaching two evenings a week and home with Penelope during the day, I actually welcomed snow days because Ethan would be home to help occupy her.

"Yiippeee!" he yelled when I gave him the news. "Let's build a snow mountain. Do you remember the one you, me, and Tommy built? That was the greatest."

Indeed, it was. The peak then was level with the roof of the garage. With all the available snow piled up between the maple tree and the back fence, the rest of the yard looked like a plucked chicken. Little tufts of brown grass poked up through the thin layer of snow left on the ground. We even had to take some snow from the alley.

"This time, let's put a flag at the top like people do when they climb Mount Everest."

Ethan sat at the table and opened a book. I turned off the radio, hoping for a moment of silence before Penelope woke up. The phone rang instead. A friend asked if his son Bryan could spend part of the day here. Another call. This time about Ethan's friend George. It would be a full house with our nephew, Beksahn, dropping in later while he waited for a ride back to school in Minnesota.

Janet came down the stairs and put on her boots by the front door. Like most working parents, she didn't have a snow day. I almost jumped out of my chair when Penelope wailed so loud the house shook.

Without looking up, Ethan deadpanned, "Mommm! Penelope's awake," sparking a guffaw from Janet, who ran upstairs to say good-bye to Penelope. After Janet left, Ethan headed upstairs to read to her until she fell asleep, as he did every day before he went to school, then returned to the basement.

An hour later, I heard a thud upstairs, followed by the pitter-patter of footsteps across the bare floor in the hallway. *Penelope was on the move.* I put the computer away as she slowly made her way down the creaking stairs. She rounded the corner clutching a baby blanket. "Gēgē?" she asked, a little blurry-eyed.

I gestured with my head toward the basement. She returned a moment later with Ethan, and I followed them upstairs into the TV room with a box of Cheerios. Pressed together on the couch, Penelope munching away on her beloved toasted Os, we watched an episode of *SpongeBob* about an itsy-bitsy character appropriately named Plankton, a favorite of ours, who aspired to be a menacing archvillain. His schemes invariably failed, however, and no one took him very seriously. Wanting to clear a beach to make room for a new location for his restaurant, the Chum Bucket, he was sitting on a tiny bulldozer with a megaphone demanding that everyone leave or he would plow them under. He screamed, but all anyone heard was barely audible squeaking. They just looked around and shrugged, which enraged Plankton.

During a commercial, Ethan gave me a knowing look with a big smile. He had nicknamed Penelope "Plankton" when she first arrived because she was the cutest little thing and yet incredibly fierce and completely unshakeable in her determination to get her way. It was meant in jest. There was nothing pitiful about Penelope, though. She was never overlooked, and with her ability to become a human hurricane at will, she was much more effective than Plankton at getting what she wanted.

After the episode ended, we went downstairs to find Bryan and his dad at the front door. Penelope and I joined the boys in the basement and played with a toy barn while they consulted about modifications to a Lego project. I glanced over at them to observe Bryan speaking. He had a gravelly voice and had the endearing habit of tilting his upper body back and a bit to the side when he spoke, particularly when he said something funny or when he was being deeply serious.

Two weeks before, Bryan had been over with another of Ethan's friends, Augie, who loved military history. After Augie left, I overheard Bryan say, as he moved several Lego figures around a fortress, "Bye-bye, Hitler. We won't miss you."

Now Bryan abruptly grabbed a Lego spaceship from Ethan, who looked back at him a bit surprised and a little hurt. Bryan spun away from Ethan and lost his grip on the ship, which fell to the floor, where it broke into pieces.

"Why did you do that, Bryan?" Ethan asked as he knelt down to try to put it back together.

"I told you to give it to me," Bryan responded, shrugging his shoulders and holding his hands out to the side, feigning innocence, "but you wouldn't. So, I had to grab it."

Sensing trouble, I said, "Hey guys, let's build the snow mountain."

We geared up and trudged through the snow holding a White Sox flag. Helping Penelope move snow with her little shovel, I watched Bryan hurl himself against the snow to pack it down. He was, indeed, a passionate kid. With his passion came a temper, which flared up from time to time, usually when you least expected it. Anger was unsettling to Ethan's gentle nature. Yet Bryan's occasional moodiness didn't seem to bother him much. He appreciated Bryan's humor and insightfulness, realizing they were of a piece with his temper.

"Bryan's not mean," he had told me once after Bryan had an episode at our house. "He's just a little rough sometimes."

"Does that bother you?" I asked.

"Not really," he responded. "He always has interesting things to say, and he is very funny, so I like him a lot. We are like brothers. We fight sometimes, but we love each other."

Ethan and Bryan planted the flag at an angle on the peak of the snow mountain and ran down together yelling, "Look out below!"

Nearing the bottom, Ethan dove into a pile of snow. Bryan slipped and fell to his left.

Standing up, laughing, Bryan said, "Dude, you are so the fun master."

They ran back to the peak and began sledding, while Penelope and I slid down the other side of the mountain on her saucer. An hour later, we made our way inside, Sylvester bringing up the rear completely covered in snow.

George and his mom were at the door. She drove off down the street; Bryan and his dad soon followed.

George and Ethan were already sledding down the snow mountain when I returned to the kitchen. Penelope stood at the big picture window, watching the boys with considerable interest. "Do you want to go outside again, Penelope?" I asked with some hesitation.

"Coldie," she said, shaking her head.

Beksahn was at the door when we entered the front room. With Penelope resting comfortably in his arms, he talked about his graduate studies in political science and his future plans. Penelope smiled and rested her tiny hands on his forearms as Beksahn spoke some Chinese with her. I was relieved she displayed no traces of the emotional unease that had prompted her to stop speaking six weeks before.

Beksahn set to work on his thesis at the dining room table when I took Penelope upstairs for her nap. He was gone by the time we returned a couple of hours later. Penelope and I ventured into the basement to find Ethan and George talking excitedly about a crucial step in a joint construction project. I sighed, sensing they were building toward asking me for an advisory opinion. They turned toward me. *Here it comes.* Speaking at the same time, they tried to explain where their visions diverged. I had no idea what they were talking about. My head was swimming from the stream of minor details that seemed earth-shattering to them. While George was talking, I noticed Penelope pick up one of their creations and begin to press one of her farm animals into it.

"*Eek!*" George screamed, as though he'd seen a mouse.

Ethan said calmly, "No, no, Penelope, that belongs over here. Let me show you."

He walked her over to the toy barn, carefully detached the farm animal, and handed the unfinished castle to George behind his back.

"Nice, Ethan," George said with a smile.

We both smiled, relieved, though for different reasons: George because he got an opportunity to finish his modification while Ethan played with Penelope, and me because I could forget about the Lego creation. That is, until I had to placate Ethan somehow about George finishing his modification without an official ruling.

Ethan was playing with Penelope when I received a text from Janet that she was on the train. Meeting her for dinner nearby, we geared up and began the trek, with me pulling Penelope on a toboggan and the boys climbing snowdrifts and throwing snowballs.

George's mom met us at the entrance and left with George. Ethan, Penelope, and I ambled into the bar, drawing curious stares from the early crowd. I stowed the toboggan, nodded at the waitress, our agreed-upon signal for a standard drink order, including Janet's, and shepherded the kids downstairs to our usual table, where other patrons would not be bothered by the kids' soaring Ethel Mermanesque voices.

Sitting at the dimly lit table, we all took a long drink. Ethan swept his hand across his mouth before saying, "Ah!" loudly. Penelope put her forearm against her mouth and looked over at him. Apparently, the first drink on a Friday mattered as much to kids as it did to me.

Ethan strode across the room and disappeared into the dark on the other side of a wood-framed opening. Penelope walked over to a chair near the opening and peered into the shadows. Suddenly, she squealed and ran back over to me. Ethan was on the floor rolling toward her, as I had done with Penelope during her speaking strike. When Ethan reached her, she tumbled over him, then righted herself, both of them laughing the entire time.

After several reiterations, Penelope stood between my legs and ate several tater tots. She then sidled up to Ethan, who put his arm around her shoulder and put his straw to her lips. He kissed her on the top of her head as she drank, and she smiled at him sweetly when she finished.

Ethan walked over to a booth in the far corner; Penelope was soon at his side. Ethan held her hand while pointing things out to her. Penelope nodded or shook her head at various proposals I couldn't hear.

At fifty, I still had the energy to play with her the way I did with Ethan when he was her age. But I was happy to defer to him. They had a special bond. He helped her feel comfortable in what was for her a very alien world. Seven months after her arrival, she was thriving in no small part because of the love he showed her.

My concern that they might not be compatible was laughable now. Like jigsaw puzzle pieces, they fit perfectly together because they were cut so differently. It was reassuring to me that they would be there for each other long after we were gone.

Penelope waved to me. I walked over and held her hand while we watched Ethan crawl into the opening at one end of an L-shaped bench.

"Penelope, I'm in here. Come find me!" Ethan called out to her from various points of the journey.

We ducked our heads under the table, with Penelope pointing as we caught brief glimpses of him in the gloom. I hurried over with her to the other end and whispered my plan into her ear. She nodded with a big smile. When Ethan emerged from the opening, I grabbed him on the tummy with a roar.

Penelope fell on top of him, exclaiming, "I got you, Ethan!"

He laughed and laughed, then told Penelope she should try it. After a nod from me, she followed Ethan through the opening. I got a little teary-eyed when I heard her little voice calling out to me, "Daddy, Daddy, I'm in here with Ethan."

18 TGiF

PENELOPE WAS BUSY TURNING my earring around slowly when I felt something brush against my arm. Ethan and his friend Matthew rushed to jump in the water, holding kickboards to their chests.

Penelope got down and pulled on my arm with surprising force. "Go," she said, pointing toward the other side of the pool.

As we passed by families at round tables, she looked over each kid, sizing up their play potential, much as Mr. Phelps in the '60s TV version of *Mission Impossible* selected agents at the beginning of each episode. It was easier in Penelope's case. The kids were so absorbed in their handheld devices, they didn't even look up. Once on the other side of the pool, Penelope pointed at Ethan, calling out, "Ethie, Ethie," as though he had been missing up until that point.

Matthew's little sister, Cynthia, appeared at our side. She and Penelope began an awkward, two-handed sword fight with noodles. I admired the effort required to wield the floppy foam floaties that were much longer than the girls were tall. The noodles then became horses, which conveyed them along the side of the pool, which was now a sea abutting a mythical land. When they weren't laughing or pointing at dragons and wizards, they made clomping and neighing sounds.

When swim class ended, Ethan grabbed a towel and walked quickly toward the locker room in a crowd of boys. He stopped at the bottom of the stairs and shook his head, sending water flying everywhere and causing his companions to call out in mock distress, "Ethan!" before they disappeared around the corner.

As I trailed the girls around the far corner of the pool, my heart sank when they saw the water dispenser, the type in dentists' offices with the tiny, single-use cone-shaped cups. It wasn't surprising they liked it so much. They had to pull hard on the cup to get it out, and it made a funny dull thud when they wrestled it free from the holder.

Normally, I would have welcomed it as a way to occupy them. The problem was it might mean an emergency bathroom stop (EBS) later. I was always grateful when a dry cleaner or some other business let us use their facilities. But some of these rivaled "the worst toilet in Scotland" in the movie *Trainspotting.* Alarm bells rang.

"Four!" Cynthia yelled.

"Yeah, four!" Penelope responded.

Four cups of water! That's the event horizon. Six meant an EBS. Five? It could go either way.

"Hey, girls. Let's go check on the boys. You can hang out on the stairs outside the locker room."

They dropped the cups immediately. I didn't know why kids liked this tiny set of stairs that led nowhere. I was just glad to have a safe place to park them for the few seconds I needed to roust the boys.

The steam room door opened as we reached the stairs. A big cloud of warm mist moved quickly across the landing and out over the pool. We lowered our heads and hurried past a portly older man to reach the first bend in the stairs to the locker room.

A miracle. Cynthia and Matthew's dad came down the stairs with the boys. And we were holding steady at four cups!

I thanked him while Ethan and Matthew huddled, talking nose to nose. The girls each had one more cup of water before we hustled out the door.

Ambling up Granville Avenue, we approached a small construction project. A pile of dirt and other materials covered by a tarp blocked half of the sidewalk a short distance ahead. Two people walked toward us from the other direction, turning the path into a catwalk.

Ethan scooted out in front of us. The wheels on the left side of Penelope's tanklike stroller ran up over the bottom slope of the debris pile. The stroller bounced and jostled over hard clods of dirt and pieces of concrete, tilting sharply downward the entire way.

"Whoa!" Penelope said, leaning forward to look down over the side like it was the edge of a deep cavern.

Once we were past the site, Ethan moved alongside me and pulled the coonskin cap he'd gotten from his cousin Joe down over his wet hair.

"You are like a stagecoach driver."

"Too bad there isn't a side rail for you to ride on," I responded, thinking how appropriate that would be given his headgear.

After we crossed Broadway, Ethan touched my arm to get my attention, something I did routinely with him because of his hearing loss.

"Hey, Dad, Matthew and I are adding a second story to the Lego spaceship that Penelope took apart."

"What's on the second story?" I asked, hoping to avoid any further grousing about the unwelcome disassembly. It had created quite a fuss. There was an animated discussion of the difficulty of putting it together without the instructions, which, not surprisingly, had gone missing in our house. Ethan's friends seemed truly upset. I'd thought then that

Ethan was hamming it up bit. He loved Penelope so much, I didn't think he could ever get truly mad at her. But he also knew siblings were supposed to fight, so he played the part of being annoyed with her.

"Well, we wanted to make it more environmentally self-sufficient," he explained. "So, we added some plants to produce oxygen. We also have a mechanic in overalls. And guess what? The mechanic speaks with a Scottish accent."

"Oh, does he now," I responded, painfully aware that I was unable to pull off the accent.

"Yeah, remember Grandpa talking about Scotsmen always being the engineers on the ships? Like Scotty on *Star Trek*," he added, with an air of uncertainty in his voice as though he'd conveyed arcane knowledge.

"Of course. The mechanic is always busy jerry-rigging things, is he?" I asked.

"There is the hyperdrive, of course. That's constantly going out," he said, "and there are a lot of gadgets that need fixing."

"Like Mom's soda maker?" I asked with a chuckle.

"That's her best gadget of all, don't you think?"

"Oh, yeah."

The week before, the top of one of Janet's home-brewed soda bottles blew off. The liquid shot up and flowed across the ceiling like a rapidly expanding fire. Soda rained down on the entire group, much to the delight of Ethan and his friends, but not the ever-sensible Penelope, who hustled to the edge of the room and waved to Janet to follow her to safety.

"Tell me more about the ship. Is Han Solo the pilot?"

"No, remember, he's on the *Millennium Falcon*."

"Oh, of course, apologies. What's the name of this ship?"

"It's still unregistered."

I was about to ask a follow-up question regarding the name when he said, "This ship has its own crew."

"Not the upright dog with the square head and the cutie-pie robots?"

"You mean Chewy? No. Besides the mechanic, there's a grandma at the helm."

"Brilliant," I said with a smile, glad to shift the discussion away from *Star Wars,* which I had unsuccessfully purged from my memory and yet still didn't remember very well. "Grandmas are definitely underutilized in our society."

"I think so too. Grandmas can do anything."

"Indeed," I said. "What we need is a grandma reserve corp. They could be called into service during disasters or other times of great need."

He laughed heartily.

"I love the innovations, feller. Very clever."

"Thanks. We had a lot of fun coming up with them. You know, now that I think about it, it is actually more fun rebuilding things without instructions."

"Why's that, buddy?"

"Well, you share ideas, and what you come up with isn't one person's idea or the other's, but both together."

"You guys don't argue about how to do things?"

"Not Matthew and me. We always seem to agree."

"I'd love to see this redesigned spaceship. Is it at home?"

"No, it's at Matthew's," he said as we turned onto our block. "I like having it there. I feel like we are always together somehow, even though we don't see each other as much as we'd like."

"That's a nice way of looking at it," I said, thinking at his age I would have insisted on some sort of joint custody arrangement.

Happily, we arrived home without an EBS. Once inside, Penelope and Ethan plopped on the couch. She leaned her head against his shoulder as he wrapped a blanket around them and began reading to her, while I scooted off to the kitchen.

I started the rice cooker, finished preparing the kale, and popped it in the oven. Sean, Theo, and Eden arrived and followed Penelope and Ethan into the basement. I cued up a Natalie Merchant CD and had a beer while I waited for the kale to finish.

I felt like I knew her personally. Long before we had Ethan, Janet and I were playing miniature golf when some kids in their late teens shyly approached us and said that Janet looked like her. When Ethan was in the NICU many years later, Janet listened to the live album repeatedly while pumping breast milk. It was an especially difficult time for her. Besides the worry about Ethan's fragile condition, she was anxious about whether he would ever bond with her. Fueling her anxiety was the cruel fact that she couldn't hold him for those first two weeks because he was in an artificially induced coma. On top of that, once conscious, his swallowing problems made it hard for him to nurse properly. Her need to connect with him was very powerful. When she was on the verge of despair, the song "These Are Days" always lifted her spirits.

I listened to it while ruminating about the kid love equivalent of a college football poll. The Penelope and Ethan polls both put Janet at number one every time. I moved up and down week by week, never higher than a strong number two, often much lower depending on who was visiting at the time. I never begrudged Janet her place in the standings, though. She devoted all her waking nonworking hours to them, and they loved her intensely in return. And yet at times she had felt she was not a good mother, that she had failed them somehow and they were not fully connected. It saddened me that a loving person like Janet, who was so well loved, had such moments of self-doubt.

There was a loud thumping sound upstairs. Two weeks before, eight-year-old Anna McCormick had suffered a gash on her forehead from the blade of the ceiling fan while playing on the bunk beds in Ethan's room. With the fan removed, I knew there could be no repeat of that particular horror. But one of Ethan's favorite stunts was still in play: jumping from the top bunk.

I hustled up to the second floor to find Eden and Penelope on the lower bunk looking through trinkets. The boys fortunately were not jumping from the top bunk; they were leaping between beds in our room. Ethan landed with his left foot on the bed, quickly pulling his right foot parallel to it like a gymnast after a dismount. After brief cheers from the small but vocal crowd out of sight to the left, he moved to the top of the bed and waved to one of the other kids to jump across. Theo executed the same move, followed by Sean.

I told them to jump only from the higher bed to the lower one and to have the nonjumpers stand on the sides of the lower bed in case the jumper stumbled. They quickly repositioned themselves and resumed.

The oven timer went off. I hurried down and pulled the kale out to cool, then ran back up to supervise the jumpathon.

They were following my instructions to the letter. Still, I remained for a few minutes out of concern for him and the others. Ethan was not a daredevil. He would never willingly put anyone else in harm's way. But his tendency to lose himself in the pursuit of fun meant that a potential mishap while playing was an ever-present possibility. Like most kids, he was always so in the moment, sometimes he didn't notice danger lurking.

Watching them, I chuckled about the way everything in our house got repurposed for some play scenario. Two queen-sized beds of differing heights in our room called out for a jumping contest. That we all slept in one room of a four-bedroom house was emblematic of our improvisational approach to life.

Penelope was quite undersized when she first arrived, coming in at the fifth percentile for height and zero percentile for weight, however that was possible. She gained weight quickly once we straightened out her diet. But she also experienced severe growing pains, spending many nights screaming and thrashing about in her sleep. We brought her into our bed in hopes of calming her down, without much success.

To make the bed less crowded, I bivouacked on the floor of the TV room for a while. I was comfortable there but quickly tired of the daily setup and teardown of my makeshift campsite. A divan chair in our bedroom was a nice alternative. It oozed coziness, and I became the envy of everyone. Both kids quickly squeezed in with me, prompting me to bring the queen-sized convertible futon sofa down from the attic. Penelope's growing pains eased, but we had already become accustomed to all sleeping in the same room, Penelope in our bed with Janet and Ethan with me.

After herding all the kids back down into the basement, I chopped onions and garlic and reflected on the makeshift quality of our lives. Janet was almost forty when she became pregnant with Ethan. We returned to the Chicago from London two months before Ethan was born and moved into our new house from a temporary apartment downtown the day before Ethan was released from the NICU. Completely occupied with Ethan's extensive medical care, we hadn't even finished unpacking by the time Penelope arrived six years later.

Even under such difficult conditions, other people might have finished unpacking, renovating, or perhaps moving to a more suitable house. Actually, I had no idea how other people seemed to live so much more sensibly than we did. I had come to realize, though, that we instinctively opted for deeper human connections over getting things done. We were more comfortable with chaos than taking time away from one another, family, friends, and even strangers. No household task or filing deadline could pull us away from having drinks with people on the front porch. The cramped bedroom, sleeping cheek by jowl, surrounded by half-read books and magazines, long-forgotten toys, unopened mail, and dust bunnies—who in their right minds would live that way? We were definitely not in our right minds, but we were okay with that.

I had finished sautéing the onions and garlic and added the fish when Janet and the other parents came through the front door. There were hugs all around. I took everyone's drink order, feeling grateful that it was finally Friday, another day we would remember.

19 Hocus-Pocus

ETHAN SPED ALONG BESIDE the beautiful Romanesque facade of Senn High School. Frisbees flew overhead, dogs ran back and forth, and kids climbed trees on the school's front lawn. An intricate set of sidewalks formed a maze perfect for bike tag. I had spent countless hours trying to corner Ethan and his friends. It was only the two of us that morning.

Ethan disappeared behind a long row of very tall bushes. I pedaled furiously toward a fork in the path. When Ethan emerged from behind the bushes, I juked toward the right fork, prompting him to turn sharply toward the left one, almost toppling over. I cut across the small strip of grass between the two paths. He looked up just in time to screech to a halt in front of my bike.

"Not fair," he said, panting. "You said we have to stay on the path."

"I know, but I'm afraid I never would have caught you otherwise."

Ethan smiled at my concession. I was relieved he was already breathing normally after such exertion. Dr. Nevin had said after his most recent pulmonary function test that his smaller airways were opening up. This was very encouraging. The floppiness of his airways and their tendency to collapse when exhaling was particularly hard to counter in the lower airways.

As Ethan grew, his upper airways still continued to collapse when he exhaled. Being larger, though, meant they were less likely to close all the way. Years of medication, activity, and relatively good health had sent rays of light into the darkness of even the deepest recesses of his lungs. I imagined it must be like being a cave dweller who finally gets some fresh air through a new crack in the wall.

Whatever joy I felt about Ethan's improving health was replaced by apprehension as we approached the crosswalk at Ridge Avenue. Drivers routinely sped right through the light. I was always a little surprised when occasionally someone stopped. Instead of red-light cameras, which would only aid in the prosecution of hit-and-run drivers, the city should install metal spike traffic barriers that pop up automatically fifty feet or so from the crossing once the light turns yellow. Pedestrians and cyclists have a much better chance of dodging a skidding car than one barreling along at forty-five miles an hour.

Safely across, we rode silently the remaining six blocks to Sister Carolyn's apartment.

"Is this our last session here?" Ethan asked as we locked up our bikes.

"For you, I believe so." Our entire family save Penelope had seen her, beginning with Janet. In fact, many people from the school and neighborhood had seen her as well, mostly with good results, after Janet shared her very favorable experience with them.

Janet was between jobs when she became concerned about her cognitive functioning. She had never been good at math, but her mathematics difficulties suddenly went from bad to worse. Not only did she have trouble doing simple calculations, but she also could not remember numbers. Her memory, generally, had also deteriorated. One day she forgot to pick Ethan up from school.

Janet thought she might have attention deficit disorder (ADD) and became worried she might not be able to hold down a job. A goodbye email from an attorney at her firm touting the right brain started her thinking in unconventional ways.

"Fight the tyranny of the left brain!" he had declared, as he went to do something more creative and sent around a link to a TED talk on the wonders of the right cranial hemisphere. An ad for brain integration technique (BIT) in the church bulletin also caught her attention. It was billed as a natural, noninvasive, lasting therapy for ADD, dyslexia, and other cognitive challenges. She decided to give it a try, figuring she had nothing to lose except for a few co-pays.

The first session involved something called muscle testing. Fans of Dr. Oz may be familiar with this, but it was completely new to me. Janet held out her arm while Carolyn asked her questions and pressed down lightly while Janet pushed up. She asked Janet to imagine a beautiful image of a tree, for example, and her arm remained very strong and did not move. However, when Carolyn asked her to do a simple mathematical calculation, her arm became very weak, and she was not able to resist the downward pressure. At one point, trying to determine if the presence of candida in her system was contributing to brain fog, Carolyn asked how many weeks Janet would have to give up sugar to rid her body of yeast. Janet, not wanting to go on a sugar fast, desperately tried to hold her arm up as Carolyn counted up from one week to eleven, but she was powerless to do so.

Finally, when Carolyn said, "Twelve weeks," the arm sprang back up.

It's hard to imagine a kookier diagnostic technique. The treatment itself, a form of acupressure, wasn't quite so magic show–like. The results, however, were miraculous. Janet began to feel better immediately, though the big fireworks occurred in the third session when she reported a tingling on one side of her head and pulsating colors on the white ceiling tiles. She became more focused, better organized, and finally able to follow through on tasks. By the eighth session, she was positively giddy as her coping abilities improved so markedly that she began to wean herself off antidepressants, an unexpected benefit of the treatments.

Most striking for me, though, was that she began seeing in three dimensions after a lifetime of only seeing in two, something she also did not expect. When she returned from Carolyn's one day, she entered the kitchen and stopped when she saw a large bag of baking soda on the counter. She walked up to the bag wide-eyed, slowly placing her hands on it as if it were a long-lost treasure, exclaiming over the beauty of its seemingly ordinary orange curves. I will never forget her face as she clutched the bag. It was a look of complete astonishment.

So now it was Ethan's turn. Carolyn greeted us at the top of the stairs with a warm smile. I half-expected her to be dressed like a fortune-teller from a B movie, or at least be wearing a wizard hat. But she remained undercover in jeans and a blue-striped collared shirt.

"Thank you for squeezing us in," I said as she showed us into the front room where her massage table was set up. Several boxes were stacked in the opposite corner of the room neatly atop one another. She was preparing to move out of state for a leadership position in her order. I marveled at how organized her place appeared even in the midst of moving. I couldn't imagine how we would ever manage to move unless a house fire or some other calamity first cleared out all the clutter.

On top of the usual move chaos, Carolyn was seeing an unusual number of patients before she left. Janet had been a bit of an evangelist for brain integration. After openly sharing her experience with others, successive waves of people from the parish and school community sought treatment with Carolyn and had similarly positive results. Now she was overrun with those seeking help. I imagined a scene from an old Frankenstein movie, where villagers with torches crowded the street outside her building, refusing to let her leave until she had treated all of them.

We finished chatting. Carolyn addressed Ethan, who sat on a little swivel chair reading. "Well, we should get started. So, Ethan, this might be your last session. Are you ready?"

He sprang to attention, saluted, and answered, "Yes, ma'am," clicking his heels for emphasis. She smiled kindly at him, while I plopped in a comfy chair opposite the stack of boxes and began to read.

I suppressed a smile while I watched Carolyn do the muscle testing on Ethan. It still seemed a little ridiculous to me that your body could tell you what it needed, even though I had experienced it myself. To keep from laughing, I recalled Janet's explanation of how it worked. Different parts of the brain fulfilled specific functions. Sometimes, though, wires got crossed, literally, as the wrong sections of the brain took on functions they shouldn't be fulfilling. The muscle testing in its various forms targeted a particular part of the brain, which was clearly overtaxed by taking on additional functions. In a sense, the brain was tricked into revealing it was trying to do too much.

How the wires got crossed was another question. For me, the likely suspect was encephalitis. In Ethan's case, it was probably one or more of the many illnesses, surgeries, or treatments he had undergone. It was anyone's guess with Janet—perhaps the stress of living with me.

After she finished testing, Carolyn moved on to the acupressure part of the treatment. By holding Ethan's head one way, then another, she applied varying degrees of gentle pressure to different parts of his skull.

After a few minutes, Ethan called out in a plaintive wail, "When will this torture session finally end?"

Carolyn smiled and looked over at me as I raised my eyebrows, a little embarrassed. Fortunately, she seemed to find it all rather funny and chuckled.

He added, "What have I done to deserve this?"

"Why don't you take a nap?" I suggested. "That's what I'd do."

"That's easy for you to say. You get to read."

"It will all be over soon," I assured him.

Several minutes passed with Ethan staring impassively at the ceiling. I put my book aside as Carolyn sat him up on the edge of the massage table.

"How do you feel?" she asked.

"Good," he responded, hunching his shoulders forward to indicate he wanted to be on his way already.

Ethan was a battle-scarred, grizzled veteran of countless medical treatments, procedures, and therapies. He had borne much of it with remarkable patience. He was especially stoic about the big things like surgeries, swallowing problems, acute and chronic respiratory difficulties, and severe hearing loss. But a half hour on a massage table with his head held gently in different positions was too much for him to bear.

After she finished the acupressure, Carolyn had Ethan stand in the middle of the small front room and asked him to execute a number of movements that he had tried to do at the outset of his therapy three months before. Some were a little uncommon, such as marching in place on a little squishy mat while touching the index finger of each hand to his nose; others were quite ordinary, like jumping jacks. These movements were meant to test whether the two sides of the brain were working well together.

"Wow, Ethan!" Carolyn exclaimed. "That's great."

It was, indeed, a remarkable difference, particularly striking with the jumping jacks. His movements were completely in sequence. He now displayed a level of coordination I hadn't thought possible for him. Even he seemed pleasantly surprised, breaking into a big smile and continuing to do them without prompting.

I didn't think that being coordinated mattered much to him. He occupied himself with imaginative play, art, music, and building models, not ball sports. Still, it must have been frustrating not being able to do what seemed like simple movements to most people.

The big relief, though, was emotional. He had developed coping problems during the previous year, which was quite uncharacteristic of him. Before this he was usually composed with a very high frustration threshold. But then he began having trouble finishing his homework, and his grades also suffered, even in subjects like art, where before he had excelled.

All this began during second grade, after Penelope had arrived. Being dethroned probably had something to do with it. He spent a lot of time visiting our neighbors, Tim and Larry, after she arrived. They said he didn't mention her at first. But then he opened up and talked about how excited he was that she was here. He was overflowing with love for her, they reported, which was evident at school as well, where he convinced many of his classmates to lobby their parents to adopt a baby from China.

I recalled how proud he was of her when she visited his classroom in her beautiful Chinese dress. Padding around in her shoes that squeaked with each step, she worked the crowd like a seasoned politician, smiling at everyone and hugging well-wishers. I was biased, of course, but I thought that she was infinitely cuter than any politician I had ever seen.

A conversation with his art teacher, Miss Phillips, confirmed more was involved than sibling rivalry. Margo had pulled me aside when Penelope and I picked Ethan up at his after-school art program and told me that she was worried about him.

"He always has a certain vision for a project, very elaborate and involving multiple complex stages. Sometimes he is not able to execute it to his specifications. He usually takes that in stride. Lately, though, he becomes inconsolable if he can't complete it that day or if something doesn't go quite as planned."

"That's not like him," I said. "I'm glad you told me. We have been a bit worried about him as well. I hope he doesn't take his frustrations out on you or the other students."

"Oh, God, no. Ethan? Never. That's the thing. He is always unfailingly kind to us and the other kids. But he has been so hard on himself lately. I just wonder if something else is bothering him."

After my talk with Margo, we walked slowly along, Ethan with his arm around Penelope's shoulder. They began a chase game on the front steps of the church, so I took a seat and watched them. After a few minutes, they sat down. Ethan read a book to Penelope while I thought about what Margo had said.

Addressing Ethan's emotional difficulties was new territory for us. I didn't know where to begin. Ethan was not prone to complain or share his feelings, at least not negative ones. Listening to him read to Penelope, I thought about how I could find out what was bothering him. Years before I would have tried the "enhanced interrogation" techniques I used to practice on Janet, which involved following her around and demanding that she tell me what was bothering her. It never really worked. In fact, it generally made her withdraw even more. Ethan would probably react much the same way.

I shook my head thinking about my feelings then. Some time ago,

I had realized my desire to "help" Janet was fueled by my intense need that she be cheerfully supportive of me. If she were occupied with her own problems, where did that leave me? I had to get her back to her old self, or what I imagined that to be, so she could hold me together.

Reminding myself I couldn't press him too hard, I said, "I know things have been a little difficult for you lately," refraining from mentioning any specifics, which might cause him to withdraw because he never wanted to speak ill of anyone.

He looked up at me sadly, then back down at his feet with tears welling up in his eyes. Penelope reached up and wiped the tears from one of his cheeks. After a group hug, he cried a bit more before saying, "It has been hard lately." The three of us sat there silently for a while. Ethan stopped crying and looked back up at me. I asked him if it would help seeing Miss Nancy. He nodded and smiled faintly.

Miss Nancy was the school counselor. Ethan had visited her a number of times after school at her house nearby, where he played bongo drums and the piano while they chatted. She said it appeared to be a great release for him. He would play single notes on the piano and let the sound fade before hitting another key, savoring the sound of each note.

The clarity of that single sound must have been soothing, partly because his hearing loss made it hard for him to sort out sounds. From my own experience with brain integration, though, I guessed it was more. For my entire life after encephalitis, extreme nervous energy coursed through my system like a high-level electric current, making it hard to concentrate. Brain integration therapy did not eliminate the current. It did reduce it noticeably, or at least its effects. I was able to control my temper more easily, I became less anxious, and my auditory memory also improved. The difference in how I felt reminded me of switching wires around on an old TV. Changing a misconnected wire reduced the feedback noise noticeably, making it more bearable.

Ethan did not talk much about how he felt after his sessions with Carolyn. It didn't matter. The changes in his demeanor after a few treatments suggested the therapy had been even more successful in his case. He was no longer so hard on himself, and his struggles at school and with homework had ended.

"Look!" Ethan beamed at me while he did another set of jumping jacks for good measure.

"Are we finished?" he asked, with fake annoyance in his voice.

"I'm afraid so," Carolyn said.

He smiled at her as she shook his hand and thanked him for being such a great patient. He thanked her and followed me down the stairs.

"It was nice of Sister Carolyn to thank me," he said as we unlocked our bikes. "But it really wasn't necessary," he added. "She's just a very nice person."

We got on our bikes and rode silently north. His reaction to what Carolyn said reminded me of when Mary Horan, the parish music director, gave him some gifts for playing the little drummer boy in the Christmas pageant two years before. He was very touched and grateful, but also a little puzzled.

"It was thanks enough to be the little drummer boy," he had said to me after she left.

I handed him a bottle of water once we came to a stop at the long light at Ridge.

"Are you glad it's over, buddy?" I asked.

He coughed a bit as he swallowed, then said, "Actually, I liked seeing Sister Carolyn. I'll miss her. She reminds me of Miss Nancy in some ways. I feel very relaxed around both of them."

"That's good."

"I guess I shouldn't have complained so much."

"She was clearly onto you."

"She does have a good sense of humor," he said, handing me back the water bottle.

Reaching toward him to grab the bottle, I noticed the countdown on the light had begun. I put the bottle in the holder. "Be ready, Ethan. The light will change soon."

"Okay," he said. "Can we go through the labyrinth again and maybe ride over to Matthew's house to see if he's there?"

I nodded. He smiled and gave me a thumbs-up.

We collected Matthew and rode off toward Senn with such frenzy it felt as though we were trying to outrun an advancing army. When we reached the school grounds, they immediately tore off in different directions. I took a third route and pursued them, quickly caught up in the chase. I sped around the narrow paths, thrilled as I tried to corner them as they frantically pedaled away in different directions. When Ethan and I crossed paths for the first time, he delightedly eluded capture. I finally cornered them after about forty-five minutes.

We continued on for another twenty minutes until they stopped, huddled together huffing and puffing near the main entrance. I suggested we call it quits. They nodded and silently rode ahead of me toward Matthew's house.

"That was great!" Ethan said after we dropped Matthew off. "And thanks for taking me to see Sister Carolyn."

"Of course, buddy. My pleasure. I hope it makes a difference," I added, thinking that if anyone needed a break in life it was Ethan.

"Me too," he said as we turned onto our alley. "Race you!" he yelled with a big laugh as he sped down the alley with me close behind.

20 A Par before Dying

THE MIDMORNING SUN SHONE through the trees lining the tee box, adding highlights to Ethan's thick mop of hair as he settled into position. He took a big swing and missed the ball entirely. Smiling, he put his hand to his forehead and pretended to look far into the distance.

Two women in their sixties were paired with us that day. The younger of the two, Maria, grinned and looked away, while Helen frowned before calling out, "You won't learn if you don't take it seriously, young man."

"Okay, buddy, try again," I said. "Just focus on keeping your head down and swinging easy."

He lined his feet up again and crouched over the ball. This time he took a nice, measured swing and hit the ball in the air about eighty yards off the forward tee. He smiled as everyone congratulated him.

Helen and Maria circled a small copse of trees in a motorized golf cart while Ethan and I waited near the large set of bunkers at the bend in the fairway. The roof of their cart got stuck under a limb. Helen was at the wheel and kept driving forward, wedging the branch more tightly on the roof. Maria was motioning to the back. Eventually they broke free, taking part of the branch with them.

Ethan's second shot didn't elevate very much, and yet it still went another fifty yards. I patted him on the back, then felt apprehensive as I noticed the ladies speeding toward us. That Helen and I had a different understanding of how to teach golf to kids was evident on the first tee. Ethan had hit his tee shot off to the right. He looked down and frowned as he walked back to his bag.

"Young man, look at me," Helen said. I assumed she was going to reassure him. Au contraire. "You need to play all your shots. It doesn't matter where you hit them, how many times you have to hit it, or how long it takes you to finish. There's no other way to learn the game. As hard as it is, you have to do it, do you understand? You'll be much better off in the long run, I can assure you."

I was stunned. I didn't want to continue the conversation, sensing a long day, but unable to leave it at that, I said, "I think the important thing is that kids try their best, make contact when possible, and enjoy themselves."

"That's precisely the problem with young people like you," she said.

"Thanks."

"For what?"

"For considering me young."

"What I mean is you have a young child. You need to raise him right, and that includes teaching him to do sports the right way."

"Okay, well, you might be right, but perhaps we should move on. We don't want to hold other people up," I added, reminding her of the rules of etiquette meant to ensure people play golf "the right way," as she put it.

It was Helen's turn. I normally would not have paid much attention to her swing. But since she introduced the topic of how to play golf, I noticed her backswing was very slow and a little truncated. But what really stood out was that her foreswing was much faster than her backswing. Of course, many people learn to control unorthodox swings very well, so I decided to reserve judgment. A dozen practice swings later, she finally appeared ready to hit. After shifting her hips back and forth a few times, she swung, hitting the ball almost directly sideways. It missed Ethan and me by a couple of feet and disappeared under a bush on the other side of the cart path.

"Are you all right?" she asked.

"Oh, yeah, we're fine," I responded, trying hard not to smile. "I see your ball. I think you will need a rescue club to hit it where it lies." I risked a smile.

"No, that's okay. Just grab it. I'll hit another," she said.

I picked up her ball and noticed her name written on it with pink marker. I tossed it to her and gave Ethan a nudge with my shoulder. Maria was smiling.

We made our way down the fairway. I was worried Helen's concern for Ethan's golf development would take all the fun out of the game. It was not like he cared much about golf. Playing together was my attempt to find an activity for him to compensate for the baseball fiasco the previous summer.

Ethan had loved T-ball, which he had played for two summers when he was five and six. Everyone got a hit, advanced the bases, and even scored. Kids learned about the game, swung a bat, fielded, and sometimes even caught balls, all without any pressure on them. This all made so much sense for a kid like Ethan who had a very cooperative nature. It didn't matter to him to be considered better than someone else. Actually, it was more accurate to say it never would have occurred to him that it mattered to be considered better than someone else.

Other parents were not so happy about T-ball's noncompetitive character. Encountering a mom from another team at the grocery store, I foolishly led with a comment about loving T-ball.

"Well, sure, if your kid isn't any good," she said.

She must have assumed since I was a coach, I shared her outlook. However, I was a coach by default. The first year I was the only person who checked the "willing to volunteer" box on the application form. The second year everyone on the team and some other parents put down my name.

The person responsible for forming teams said, "You must be a really great coach. So many people said they want to be on your team."

She didn't realize my only qualification was that I hosted happy hours before the games.

"I mean, if no one gets out and everyone scores, what's the point?" the baseball mom at the grocery store asked.

"Fun?" I suggested tentatively.

"Hah!" she said. "What's fun about that? How can you tell who's better?" she added with raised eyebrows. "That's why we can't wait for coach pitch. Start sorting kids out."

Sorting out. *Don't you do that with produce, not kids?*

"Are you guys going to do coach pitch?" she asked.

"I'm not sure. Ethan likes T-ball a lot, but I'm not sure coach pitch is right for him."

"Well, you'll know pretty quickly," she had said before walking briskly down the aisle in the opposite direction.

Back at the golf course, I was rummaging in my bag when Ethan yelled, "Look out!" Helen's errant shot almost grazed my left shoulder.

"Sorry," she said as they whizzed by us and headed up a small hill at the edge of the sand trap.

We looked at each other wide-eyed. "Would you like to ride with them rather than walk?" Ethan shook his head emphatically.

We watched them traverse the next fairway in all directions looking for their ball. Then, Ethan hit a couple of shots toward the green while we waited for them to find their balls and hit.

My mind drifted back to the conversation with baseball mom at the grocery store. I had spent the rest of that day thinking about what I should do about the upcoming season. Her emphasis on sorting kids out, as she put it, made me inclined to not sign him up the following year.

I decided not to mention coach pitch to him in hopes that the deadline might pass unnoticed. Big mistake. I should have made the decision for him. I could have emphasized all the time we'd have in the evening to do other things. By waiting, I lost the initiative. He had come home from school one day all aflutter about playing after talking with his friends about it.

Helen and Maria roared around the sand trap to our right and sped toward the green, coming to a stop with a skid near the ball washer on the next tee. They slowly made their way over the hill behind the green and searched for their balls in the deep grass along the fence.

I told Ethan that he could take a break at the next tee if he was quiet and stayed out of our way. He scampered off with his bag through the gap between the green and the sand trap, toward a bench in the deep shade.

My second shot landed on the right side of the green about twenty-five feet from the hole. Walking to the green, I recalled that fateful first game of coach pitch. It was right on the heels of a big birthday party. On the way to the game, Ethan seemed so tired that I thought we should skip the game. I felt obligated to go, however. I was the assistant coach because once again I had checked the volunteer box.

After we finished setting everything up, I suggested to the coach that Ethan sit out. He agreed, saying he could go in later if he felt better. Suddenly, though, one of the people who hadn't checked the volunteer box took the clipboard, started managing the lineup, and ignored my request to keep Ethan out of the game.

"If he's here, he plays," he said emphatically while walking away.

Pleased to be relieved of duty, I was still uneasy about Ethan playing that day. I went up and asked him if he wanted to try, and he said yes. I decided to see how it went. It was wrong to interfere, I told myself, when someone has taken on an assignment, particularly a volunteer one. I assumed the role of chief cheerleader.

Many parents were excited when their child went up to bat. This was "their" moment to shine in the public eye. Baseball provided a particularly good stage, as much of the game focused on what transpired between pitcher and batter, and after the pitch was thrown all eyes were on the batter. No wonder parents hovered around the guy with the clipboard, anxious to find out when their child was up.

The way baseball focused all eyes on the batter was not good for Ethan. In fact, it was potentially disastrous. His noncompetitive nature relieved him of the common human foible of a fear of failure. The problem was he didn't like to be the center of attention, and he didn't want to disappoint people. I watched him bat, hoping he would make contact, not because I wanted him to be "sorted" out with the good players but because I knew he would feel like he let his teammates down if he didn't get a hit.

He struck out three times, becoming more withdrawn each time. By the end, he was sitting by himself on the ground with his back against the fence with tears in his eyes. I should have left him alone with his feelings. Instead, I told him it didn't matter whether he got a hit or not. He could still be a good teammate by sitting with the other players and cheering for them. Eventually, he did. One player was particularly nice to him; Ethan seemed to appreciate his kindness. Our good friend Megan's son, Ryan, who was on the other team, also came up to him to offer some encouragement. Still, he was clearly dejected.

As we walked to the car after the game that day, I knew I should let him have his feelings. But my mouth was pressing to the fore, ready for action. I continued my lecture about being a good teammate, despite being vaguely aware it was the wrong thing to do. At some level, I seemed determined to make the entire baseball experiment a parental failure of epic proportions. I knew I'd succeeded when he had looked up at me with teary eyes and said, "I guess I'm not a good Dodger."

I was a lock for inclusion in the pantheon of bad parents.

I felt a tap on my arm. Helen gestured toward Ethan, who was looking at some stones on the little hill behind the fairway bunker.

"He should be playing all his shots from precisely where they lie."

Years of unsolicited parenting advice had made me quite thick skinned. Normally, I would have just ignored her. She wasn't any worse than the countless other people, who had tried to mentor me without my consent. At that moment, though, still so angry at myself for having failed Ethan, I was defenseless. She was able to push me over the edge. "Try worrying about your own game instead, which, by the way, needs a lot of improvement," I barked at her.

Speechless, she walked off shaking her head.

"Oh, by the way," I called out, "what club did you use to hit your ball out of the bushes on the first tee?"

Maria smiled while Helen prepared to take her next shot. After several practice swings, she ambled over to her bag to select another club. Meanwhile, Ethan ran over to a tree with some low-hanging branches a few yards behind her and to her right. By the time she had returned with a different club, Ethan had already climbed eight or ten feet above the ground and waved at me with a smile. Climbing trees was his favorite part of playing golf.

Please, please, please turn around, I silently willed Helen. *Damn!* She hit her ball and walked away without noticing him.

After I finished the hole, Ethan made the sign for a Subway sandwich. I nodded, prompting him to scamper up to me and hug me around the midsection. As we walked toward the next tee, I told him we would play this hole and perhaps one more.

Ethan accompanied me up the steep incline to the tee box and stood silently while I prepared to tee off. I hit my drive to the left edge of the green. Maria ended up about twenty yards short of the green with a good approach to the pin, while Helen drove into the front side of the yawning sand trap that wrapped most of the way around the green.

The three of us waited together as Ethan set up to hit. "Is that high enough?" he asked, knitting his brow.

"That's great, buddy," I responded. As he took a couple of practice strokes, I noticed how smooth his swing had become. All the wrangling with the golf oracle had distracted me from how well he was playing.

He paused for a moment before swinging, watching the flight of a beautiful butterfly a few feet away. "Did you see that, Dad?"

"It's beautiful, Ethan. But try to concentrate and hit the ball."

He watched it a second longer, then turned his gaze to the ball. If he took much longer, I feared Helen might say something. I was relieved when he began his backswing. Everything looked great. His left arm was straight. He brought his arms up to their fullest extension. The club was parallel to the ground at the top. His foreswing was the same speed as his backswing. He shifted his weight nicely and pivoted gracefully as he swung through the ball. Most importantly, he kept his head down until his follow-through naturally brought his head up.

There was dead silence. I felt as if I was witnessing something magical, and perhaps Helen and Maria did as well. He had hit a number of balls quite well. But none like this one. His ball was arcing straight for the green without any left or right movement. When we had all caught our breath, we marveled at the shot and let out a collective, "Ohhhh," as it landed at the front of the green to the right of the hole. The downslope of the green caused the ball to break quite a bit left as it rolled about another ten feet. Finally, it stopped about five feet directly below the hole. It was hard to imagine a better shot.

"That was fabulous, Ethan!" I said. "Your swing was perfect, and your shot was beautiful. How did it feel?"

"Good," he replied matter-of-factly.

"After the next hole, do you want to play more?" I asked, thinking he might after that shot.

"Sure, if you want. But I am getting a little hungry."

I nodded, happy to honor a long family tradition. My siblings and I often played golf with Uncle Sunny and Grandma Chee Chee. Near dusk, Sunny would drive us down into the middle of the country club in his big Chrysler. We played about three or four holes until it got dark, then headed off to a bar to eat footlong hot dogs and onion rings and play an arcade bowling game with tiny balls and little plastic pins.

We still had to finish the hole, of course. Once we were all on the green, I marked Ethan's ball since he was closest to the pin. Everyone finished putting to give Ethan the spotlight for his birdie attempt. I put his ball down and turned to talk to him about his putt, but he was crouched over something at the edge of the green. "Look at this bug. It's huge."

It was a beetle, and it was, indeed, enormous. Very dark brown, rounded back, huge pinchers at the front, with several thick pairs of legs, it moved slowly across the short-cut grass of the green.

He was so absorbed in charting the creature's movements that the significance of the moment was completely lost on him.

"It's a very interesting bug, Ethan, but we need to finish up."

"But someone might step on it or a ball might roll over it," he objected.

"We can't worry about that now. When we finish the hole, we'll put it in the trees."

"Okay," he said, while the insect equivalent of an M1 tank continued its slow trek across the green.

I handed Ethan his putter. Crouching over the ball, he turned and peered over his shoulder to check on the bug. He clearly wouldn't be able to concentrate until he knew it was safe, so I said, "Ethan, I promise you. I will watch the bug, and we will get him to safety. Just finish your putt."

He looked once more over his shoulder before hurriedly hitting the ball. It hopped after he hit it, sending it a bit off-line. Rolling by the cup an inch to the left, it came to rest three inches past the hole. A fine attempt, really. With a downhill lie, though, it was still a difficult comebacker despite the short distance. Knowing his mind was still on the beetle, I walked up and tapped the putt into the hole, prompting Helen to remind me of the importance of Ethan taking all his shots. I ignored her and looked over at Ethan, who had dropped his putter and was kneeling over the bug, as though it were a dying relative.

I said goodbye to the ladies, wishing them well. Ethan waved at them as they drove off to the next tee. I was relieved Helen didn't try to give Ethan some parting advice. Perhaps even she sensed that it would not have registered.

I picked up Ethan's putter and bag. He looked at me hopefully. I nodded, and he scurried over to a tree with the bug in hand. I beamed with pride watching him place it on a limb with great care. When he turned toward me smiling, he reminded me of my dad, also a gentle soul, who often stopped play to pick insects up off the tennis court and carry them to safety.

As we walked together, I marveled at Ethan's modesty. He had his first par, and it didn't matter to him. The highlight of the day, what he would remember, was encountering and relocating the bug.

I peered up the hill to the seventh tee. No one was ready to tee off, so we went down to number eight. I told Ethan to take his bag over to the tree to the right of the green and wait for me. He was thrilled and hurried over as fast as he could with his bag dangling back over his hindquarters. It was a great climbing tree, arguably the best in the whole course. The trunk grew out of the ground on one end and arched up and over before reentering the ground about fifteen feet in the other direction.

After I finished the hole, we walked up the ninth fairway talking the about the bug. Once in the car, we both fell silent. He became immersed in his book, and I turned on the radio, which was tuned to a sports talk radio station. Two guys were wrangling about what would happen at the trade deadline in Chicago. I remembered him as a five-year-old pointing out that people on sports talk radio said the same things over and over, only a little different each time.

"Why don't you play the beautiful music instead?" he had asked then.

Yeah, why not? I turned the dial to the classical station.

They were playing Beethoven's Sixth Symphony. The third movement ended as I pulled to a stop in the Subway parking lot across from the Rosehill Cemetery. Ethan looked up from his book when the fourth movement began and asked, "Hey, isn't that Beethoven?" I caught his eye in the mirror and nodded. "That was in the Barbie movie we watched with Penelope last night," he added.

"Yeah, you're right," I said, while I recalled how cozy they looked together, Penelope nestled comfortably on his lap on the couch in the basement.

"How 'bout we listen to it for a minute?" he asked.

"Sure, buddy," I responded, content to enjoy the view of the beautiful cemetery on the other side of the busy boulevard.

"And maybe we can watch the movie again with Penelope when we get home," he suggested.

"That would be great." Settling back into my seat, I whispered, "This sure beats sports talk radio."

21 The Sing Sing Thing

ETHAN BOWED AND BELTED out the customary greeting, "OSS!" when we entered the dojo. The lobby was packed with parents and kids jockeying for position, some trying to leave, others to make it to class. With several nods and smiles, we found our way through the crowd and slipped off our shoes.

Ethan went to change while Penelope and I looked for a seat in the viewing area. It was already full, so we sat on the floor in the wide middle aisle. Usually, we watched only the first few minutes of class before stepping out. That day, however, I wanted to stay longer to see how Ethan was doing.

The week before, the instructor, Senpai Peggy, had asked to speak with me about an incident in class. As we moved into a little office near the front desk, I braced myself to hear about Ethan not paying attention or goofing around too much in class.

After a pause, she said, "I think you should know about something that happened in class today. Another boy kept pulling on Ethan's hearing aids," she added, before glancing over at Penelope, who watched her intently. "Ethan asked him to stop several times. 'It's important,' he had told him, but the boy wouldn't let up. Eventually, I had the other boy sit with his parents and asked them to move out of visual range, so as not to unsettle Ethan."

"I'm sorry I wasn't there," I said, uncertain what I would have done anyway.

"It's fine. We don't expect parents to always be there. And it's probably best if we try to handle it first."

"No argument there," I said, relieved, knowing I probably would have overreacted. "It sounds like a very difficult situation, but you handled it quite well."

"Thanks," she said, looking over at Penelope, who held out her arms to her. I passed her over to Peggy. Penelope cupped Peggy's face in her hands and looked her over closely, then turned toward me with her arms out, and I took her back.

Peggy continued, "Fortunately, the other family was quite good about it. But the really impressive thing was Ethan's reaction. Boys his age in that circumstance often react physically. He was firm, though polite. He remained composed and continued in the class and did quite well."

"I'm glad to hear that," I said, a little surprised. I wouldn't have expected Ethan to hit him or shove him. He had too gentle a spirit for that. It was more likely for him to become pouty and have trouble continuing in the class. "It's great that everything was resolved amicably and that he didn't sulk for a while."

"And," she said, "I was very touched that he thanked me for helping him."

"He should be grateful," I said. "You did him a great service. He doesn't feel embarrassed about wearing hearing aids," I added, pausing to knock on the wooden doorframe. Penelope leaned out to tap the frame, smiling with a nod. "But he does get tired of talking about them. It's been a while since kids have pulled on them, so he was probably taken by surprise. I'm relieved that he reacted calmly and let you handle it, and that you were able to defuse things so effectively."

Senpai Peggy was teaching the class again this week. She nodded in our direction as she positioned herself in front of the group. Sitting on the floor with Penelope in my lap, I surveyed the kids in the class, wondering if the perp was there. It was probably best not to know. There was no doubt a metaphysical limit on the number of times you can cast a hairy eyeball at someone else's kid without spiritual consequences, and I was sure I'd already exceeded it.

Scanning the crowd, I wondered if any other parents struggled. I often had the impression that parenting was not difficult for them. Then I would witness a meltdown, or someone would confide in me, and I'd realize they, too, were challenged. What I found inspiring was that in the midst of it all, people could be very thoughtful and kind.

I was particularly touched by a little girl in Ethan's class. She'd noticed his hearing aids and gave him a children's book about a bunch of kid detectives, each of whom had a special ability they could use to catch bad guys. One had hearing aids and could use his FM trainer to spy on the teachers, so they all knew when it was safe to sneak out and do their sleuthing.

Sometimes Ethan did know what the teachers were talking about when they were out of the room because they occasionally forgot to switch off the FM trainer. He even overheard them in the bathroom on occasion, which gave him considerable street cred among primary school chums.

I was so grateful to this little girl and her family for planting the idea in our heads that Ethan's hearing aids gave him an edge. As far as I knew, he never put this unintended feature of his hearing aid technology to use as a grade school PI. He did have an excellent sense of humor, though, that endeared him to his classmates as they slogged through long school days together, and the FM trainer provided him some great material.

One day, he famously announced on the playground, "Prepare yourselves for a math quiz after recess everyone. It's coming!" That's when he and Theo became fast friends, and they had been inseparable ever since.

Penelope and I went into the boys' locker room after class. Often being the only dad on site, Sarah, one of the dojo directors, had asked me to supervise the boys to make sure things weren't getting too out of hand. As I rounded the corner holding Penelope, I had to duck to avoid being hit in the face by a pair of pants. Penelope pointed at two boys completely covered in clothes. Another kid was working his way into a locker near the front door.

After a few minutes of me pulling kids out of lockers, Penelope and I herded the boys into a circle at the center of the room. They sat there slowly putting on their clothes and laughing themselves silly at their jokes, which I could not begin to understand. I breathed a sigh of relief as they started to filter out of the locker room. We walked out, and I told the last two moms waiting at the door that their boys were almost dressed.

While driving home I thought about how much better things were at karate the second time around. We had taken a break because Ethan was having difficulty concentrating in class. Janet thought he might be too young for a class after school. The hiatus offered me a face-saving way to abandon my efforts to disprove her theory that lecturing kids about their behavior was ineffective. I shifted uneasily in my seat as I recalled scolding him when he goofed around in class and contributed to locker-room pandemonium. Afterward, I always drove home fuming, while he became lost in his book.

Next time there, it happened all over again; the parental anger version of the movie *Groundhog Day*. A year later, he was much more focused in class and kept the locker room hijinks to a minimum. *What a difference a year makes.*

Once at home, I prepared dinner, and the kids settled into the living room. Our friend Anne's babysitter, Jana, had taught me that doing housework was a great way to get some alone time. Unfortunately, it didn't work as well with Penelope as it did with Ethan. When she wanted your attention, she was going to get it no matter what your plans were. Nothing got done, and she could go on indefinitely like a Senate filibuster during the civil rights era. She sometimes woke up the next day and continued her tantrum.

"Do exactly what I say, and no one will get hurt," we imagined her saying.

I shook my head thinking about how much worse I had handled Ethan's tantrums, even though they were far less intense than Penelope's. I typically became angry that I would have to wait him out or give him a time-out, derailing whatever we were doing. Janet said over and over, don't take it personally, remain calm, give him a time-out, and be done with it. I usually opted for an adult tantrum, stomping around yelling, lecturing him about how he should behave. It was like two toddlers in a cage match on a professional wrestling show, though from two radically different weight classifications.

I poured myself another glass of wine and paused at the sink before calling them to the table. Ethan was commenting on one of Penelope's drawings.

"You should call it 'Tornado Attack,' Penelope," he said, and wrote the title at the top of the page.

I nearly spit out a mouthful of wine as I thought about how Penelope's tantrums were like being swept up into a tornado. Ethan loved Penelope's feistiness, even her tantrums.

"Ohhhhh, Penelope," he would say with a smile and a laugh when she screamed about something, thoroughly charmed by her determination to get her way.

Janet came through the back door. Rushing home from a meeting downtown with her new boss, she was in such a hurry to get inside to see the kids that she forgot to take off her bike helmet. Ethan hugged her around the waist. I stood behind him holding Penelope, who placed both hands on her helmet, smiled, and shook her head, apparently not fully supportive of Janet's choice of headgear. The three of them sat on the living room couch and discussed future birthday plans while I watched them from the entryway.

I was happy for Janet. In a couple of weeks, she would be starting a new job as the library manager in a major law firm. It was hard for her at first being furloughed after twenty-five years at the same firm. There was worry about finding a job, even the possibility of relocation to another city. Before too long, though, she came to see that being a casualty of the global economic meltdown was also an opportunity to reset her career and her life. Never fully comfortable as an executive, she was delighted to be returning to the library. Her true love was information. Making it available to others was more fulfilling than ordering other people around and deciding their fates.

It also seemed likely her hours would be much more manageable, giving her more time for herself and for us. And there was so much that she needed and wanted to do. Her entire life, for example, she had struggled with double vision. After surgery five years before only made it worse, she started vision therapy to help her control it more effectively. With her schedule, however, it was hard to make the appointments regularly and practice effectively. Maybe she could do that now. There was a whole slew of other things she would like to do—study alternative medicine, read, attend lectures, exercise regularly, and, most importantly, spend more time with Ethan and Penelope.

Most people wouldn't notice a change. Her powerful instinct to make people happy induced her to downplay, sometimes even conceal, her own personal struggles. I was often fooled. How could I forget she had double vision? I had seen her bloody, devil movie-eyes after the surgery, was there as it became clear the surgery did not work, watched her practice compensating for the condition, and knew about the many different types of lenses she had tried over the years. And yet I was surprised when she sometimes could not bring her eyes into alignment. *Oh, right, double vision.*

To an outsider, she would still be the ever-cheerful, nurturing person they all loved. I, too, was an outsider once. Her positive outlook fooled me into believing she didn't need anything. As I became less touchy and controlling, she was more comfortable showing me her authentic self, sometimes tired and stressed, other times angry and frustrated, yet always loving.

It took time for me to learn how to sense what she needed and how best to respond. Sometimes this meant not doing anything, just letting her be comfortable with her feelings and allowing her to express them. The German television translation of the iconic phrase from American cop shows, "Freeze!" often flashed through my mind in these circumstances—*Keine Bewegung*! literally, "No movement!" It was hard to say how things would change after she started the new job. My goal was to remain agile and help her find her way under the new circumstances.

After dinner, Ethan and I went to basketball practice. In a crowd of people waiting for the gym to open, a kid named Tyler stood next to Ethan. I had major issues with this kid. The year before I had invited him to go to a movie with Ethan and Will, another classmate of Ethan's, and Will's older sister, Madison. The whole thing was my idea, not Ethan's. We hung out with Will's parents, Susie and Jim, quite a bit. When Ethan and Will were younger, they played well together at our gatherings, especially at our house, which Will described as "totally awesome." More recently, Will was at times a little moody and didn't want to play with Ethan. He wasn't so much mean as just not very interactive. I thought if they did more together in between our social events, they might develop play routines. Ethan didn't seem to be bothered by Will's aloofness. He certainly didn't say anything about it. It was mostly my uneasiness about Ethan perhaps feeling bad when Will didn't want to play with him. So I volunteered to take our kids on outings during school in-service days, when Will's parents were working.

We had done this several times before, and it went very well. So I was surprised the day before the outing when Ethan said to me, "You'd better also invite Tyler to the movie."

"Why?" I responded, truly puzzled. Ethan and Tyler had played some when they were younger. His mom and sometimes his dad would stop on their way somewhere and exchange pleasantries while the boys played on the sidewalk. Ethan and Tyler ended up in pre-school together, but they didn't play very much with each other as far as I knew. Normally, I would not have been concerned about it. Not everyone connected. But I began hearing things about Ethan's class in preschool that concerned me a little.

Ethan was part of a large group of kids who spent most of their free time together. My impression was that it wasn't exclusive. In fact, a couple of the boys and a little girl had some problems making friends and feeling accepted, which suggested all were welcome in the group. I wondered, though, when another parent told me that his son felt excluded.

I didn't see there was much I could do other than encourage Ethan to be more inclusive. We already had playdates at our house with many of the kids in the class, boys and girls alike, and even hosted the entire preschool and kindergarten for several playdate/happy hours. Still, I invited the boys not part of Ethan's friend group for playdates so they wouldn't feel left out. Maybe if they played with Ethan individually, it would be easier for them to integrate themselves into the group, if they wanted to be involved. Tyler was one of those kids. When I invited him, his mother declined, saying, "He really doesn't like that sort of thing."

Then this two years later? Walking home from school, I asked Ethan about it.

"He said he'd kill me if I went to a movie alone with his friend."

I was stunned. Before I could respond, we ran into Ethan's friend Joey, also known as "Cheese." They veered off into the alley and ran up to the "fly bush," as they called it, stirring up a huge swarm of giant black flies. While they bobbed and weaved to avoid the flies, I shared a laugh with Joey's mom about their food nicknames. Ethan's was "Crackers." It had all started between Joey and Ethan at lunch one day. Before long, everyone in the class had one. It was a seemingly inexhaustible source of laughter for the entire class.

We parted after a few minutes. Watching them walk away, it occurred to me that Ethan didn't use jokes, stories, and pranks to distinguish himself or put other people down. Humor, for him, was a way to connect with people and be inclusive. I was very proud of him for that.

Walking down the alley toward our house, I asked him again about what Tyler had said.

"Yeah, he thinks I'm trying to take his friend away."

"I don't get it," I said. "We're only going to a movie."

"I know. I told him that. But he's pretty insistent."

"Maybe I should cancel everything."

"No," he had said. "I think it's easier to invite him."

I spoke with Janet about it before bedtime. "Kids are territorial," she said matter-of-factly. "You've taken Will on outings a few times. Tyler obviously feels a little threatened."

"It's second grade, not Sing Sing prison," I said, "though, now that I think about it, kid world is a lot like prison life. Besides the regimentation and lack of freedom, kids need to be connected and to protect their turf."

"That's true. It is a bit primitive, but we are all animals, after all. Remember, according to the author of *1-2-3 Magic*, you are not a parent, you're a wild animal trainer. Just make clear what behavior is acceptable and enforce it."

"If I am a wild animal trainer," I asked, "can I use a whip?"

She laughed and gave me a kiss. "It will be fine. If not, you can stop with the outings. Why do you need other kids along anyway? Isn't that more of a bother?"

Unhelpful, as always, I thought as I watched her walk into Ethan's room. I knew she was right. It would be easier with just Ethan. Being an extrovert myself, I had always assumed that he wanted other kids his age along. But he seemed happy to do things with just me or with me and Penelope.

I went into Ethan's room. He and Janet were cuddled in the small lower bunk. I knelt down and said, "I'm worried about him saying he would kill you if you didn't invite him."

"He doesn't really mean it. He just really wants to come along."

"Okay," I said. "We'll see how it goes."

"Thanks. It will be okay, I promise."

Wait, isn't that my line? I gave both of them a kiss and started to climb in between them. "No," he said, with his throaty chortle. "There's not enough room."

"Okay," I said. "But next time, I'm joining you." I smiled as I got up and walked to the back room to call Tyler's parents.

Ethan was so excited when I picked them up the next day. He ran up to Will and Tyler exclaiming about how much fun they were going to have. Tyler stood between Ethan and Will with his back turned to Ethan, trying to ignore him. As we walked home, he kept pushing Ethan away, saying, "Go away," "Stay away from us," and "Don't walk with us." It didn't seem to occur to him that if Ethan went away, the guy with the driver's license and wallet would go with him. He kept at it even after I told them there would be no movie if such behavior continued.

If this is a kiddie Sing Sing, why can't I just shank them?

I felt trapped, though was I really? I could have called the parents and sent them on their way. But I didn't want to have to tell them the kids were being mean.

Suddenly, I imagined Janet saying, "You could simply say they weren't up for the movie or that they wanted to be on their own. If the parents press for an explanation, just say, 'Well, there were some behavior issues.' No specifics. Trust me, they won't want to know more."

The rest of the outing went pretty much as it began. Fortunately, Ethan took it all very well. He got a little teary-eyed once, but only very briefly. At lunch and the movie, he sat with Madison and me. Very quickly he was his cheerful self. When we got home, he threw himself fully into a snowball fight that ended very quickly for the other two boys, who were in tears because their hands got cold. Madison kindly took them inside while Ethan and I played in the snow a bit longer.

As we walked toward the house, I apologized to him for bringing Tyler along. "It's okay," he said with a smile. "I still had a good time. Thanks for taking me. Can we see it again?"

"Yeah, that would be great."

"But can we take Penelope this time? She would love that movie."

"Great idea, buddy," I responded, relieved and grateful for his instinctive ability to see light in the darkest situations.

A light came on behind me. Someone had opened the storage room to search for keys to unlock the gym. After a gentle tap on my shoulder, I moved aside to let someone pass and noticed Ethan still standing next to Tyler along the wall to my left. It was very hard not to give him the evil eye after that movie outing.

In the midst of my fretting, Ethan turned to Tyler and asked, "Hey, do you want to practice passing?"

Tyler looked as surprised as was I. "Sure," he said, and they began passing back and forth to one another until the doors opened.

After I found a seat in the gym to watch practice, I thought about the exchange with Tyler. Ethan could easily have just stood there without speaking. Yet he was willing to take a chance and reach out to the kid. Whether or not it was his intention, Ethan gave Tyler an opportunity to be better, to make amends by behaving differently. And he did.

I watched the kids running drills. Ethan was in a group with a boy named Johnny. He was one of the best players on the team and, according to Ethan, a very nice kid. I marveled how he tore around the court and executed his assignments so deftly. My fascination wasn't due to his speed or skill level so much as that he was running at all. As a playground monitor in first grade, I had been a little surprised when Johnny's mother suddenly began showing up, even though she didn't need to be there. Later, I learned that Johnny had a condition affecting his bones. He would grow out of it, but for quite a while he wasn't allowed to run. How torturous that must have been for him and his family. They all seemed very athletic, so that must have felt like the kid activity version of the Nazi Schreibverbot, where a soldier stood guard to make sure someone didn't write in any form, even a shopping list. *We all suffer.*

My attention returned to Ethan. He didn't care much about sports. We had told him he needed to do something physical and that basketball wasn't a bad thing to learn. "It is a great way to socialize," I said. "Look how older kids, boys and girls, will get together to shoot baskets in the alley." He was persuaded.

Basketball was difficult for him, though, especially before he became more coordinated after his brain integration therapy. It was also hard in a noisy gym for him to hear his teammates and coaches, even with digital hearing aids. To help him cope, I practiced passing with him in the alley and told him to pass the ball whenever he got it in a game. That's exactly what he did. Even after gaining more hand-eye coordination, he was still not interested in shooting. This made him a valued teammate, especially to the guys who only wanted to shoot.

I glanced at the court, where Ethan shared a laugh with his good friend Freddie before they were herded into separate groups. The coach was turned away from Ethan as he talked. Coupled with the poor acoustics in the gym, Ethan probably couldn't hear what the coach said. There was also a big kid in Ethan's group yelling at other players. After the last practice, Ethan had said, "He thinks I am some sort of disease." I guessed from his demeanor that he thought that of many kids.

Everyone began moving in sequence. Suddenly, the mouthy kid passed the ball to Ethan, who was looking the other way, and yelled at him when he missed the ball. Ethan nodded. As he walked back to his position, Ryan, one of the better players on the team, stopped him to offer some words of encouragement, prompting Ethan to smile. The next time the ball came his way, Ethan was prepared. He caught it and passed it along as he was expected to do.

"Wow," I said softly to myself, not because I was impressed by the pass he made but because he seemed so unfazed after being yelled at by a teammate. I shook my head thinking that at age nine, I would not have responded so well.

"You did great tonight, Ethan," I said while driving home.

"Thanks," he responded, looking up at me with a smile. "I thought it was fun. I know I'm not great at basketball, but I like being part of the team. Thanks for getting me to play."

I nodded, struck by how far ahead of me he was emotionally at his age. He wasn't alone. Countless times in the last ten years, I had been taken aback by how wise many kids were at such a young age.

In preschool, for example, Ethan had been absent for a couple weeks with pneumonia. When he returned, he wanted to sit next to his friend George and refused to sit next to a girl named Sade. He liked Sade, but he missed his friend so much he couldn't help himself from protesting.

It was the Sing Sing thing all over again. Ethan had been a little isolated at his previous preschool after an extended absence. At a new school, he had found a friend he dearly loved, and then he missed school for two weeks due to another illness. He had probably felt threatened and worried he would lose his friend. *Perhaps Tyler felt the same way.*

My mind returned to the incident with Sade. Mrs. Harrington called me, and I took him home. He didn't want to leave, of course.

He cried a little as I firmly held his hand and marched him out of the school.

"I am sorry to hurt Sade's feelings," he said while we sat together on the benches in front of our house. "I will say sorry tomorrow."

Waiting for a pedestrian to cross before turning onto our block, I remembered Sade's response to his apology.

"That's okay, Ethan," she said. "You know, you can be best friends with George. But we can still be friends too."

Right on, sister.

It was raining hard when we arrived at our house. "Are you ready to make a run for it?" I asked.

Ethan nodded, and we scampered to the cover of the front porch. As we walked into the house, I thought about how lucky I was to get the chance to learn so much from all these kids. *I hope I reach adulthood before they do.*

22 The Long Goodbye

ON A HOT DAY in mid-August, two weeks before Ethan entered fourth grade, I sat with Penelope and her friend George on the shore of Lake Michigan. They were making preparations for a royal wedding. The sandcastles were finished, but there was so much still to do. A small flotilla waited offshore, ready to dock. The dignitaries on the boats were, well, indignant about being kept waiting. Apparently, there was a problem with the wedding dress. George was moving a small boat across the sea to retrieve a new one while Penelope reviewed seating arrangements with one of the queen's servants.

I felt wistful watching them play. Summer days have just as many seconds, minutes, and hours as any other time of the year. Yet every spring, there is time displacement effect, where standard units of time seem elongated as I think about the impending summer, encouraging me to make grandiose plans. That year was no exception. In addition to brushing up on French and building a new set of stairs for the back deck, I would complete the research on a book about John Dewey at the University of Chicago Library and continue the Pilates classes I had started in the winter, along with all the other exercise and reading I did routinely.

Then, Ethan dropped a bomb right before the school year ended. He didn't want to do any summer camps.

"It's not that summer camps aren't fun," he said. "It's just they are a bit of grind, a little too much like school. And they keep me from doing other stuff like writing cartoons and spending time with my friends."

Points all well taken. I was fine with postponing research on the book. Why would I spend time in a library on beautiful summer days anyway? But I *really* wanted to continue the Pilates classes, which had been a bit of a revelation to me. My "mild" CMT symptoms were no longer so mild. My feet and ankles were getting worse despite my rigorous training and new orthotics from the CMT clinic. The stronger core muscles I developed via Pilates enabled me to hold my body more erect and stand and walk more squarely on my feet. I experienced much less pain and had fewer leg cramps, even though I spent less time stretching. I *had* to continue the classes.

No worries. I had a plan. Ethan and I could bike there together on the two days a week Penelope spent in day care. He could read in the kids' gym during the class, and we could have lunch at some fun place afterward. Best of all, the hour-long round trip combined with the class would be just enough exercise for the day, freeing up more time to work on the book.

The well-laid plan assumed the tandem bike we had inherited from a friend was in good working order. It was not. Its frame was bent slightly, causing it to angle left with the front wheel wobbling a bit. That was fine for short jaunts in the neighborhood, but not the long ride to the health club. Ethan had outgrown the tagalong bike, so we would each have to ride our own bikes there.

"A nine-year-old could definitely ride safely down Clark Street past Wrigley Field to the Lakeview neighborhood," my desiring-self told my better-self. An intra-self-compromise was reached. We would experiment on a side street first.

"I am not comfortable riding in the street," Ethan called out after we had gotten a couple of blocks from our house.

I glared at him. Anger welled up inside me as the last piece of my summer plan disintegrated like a vampire at sunrise.

"I'm sorry," he said, teary-eyed. His voice quavered and his shoulders shook. "But I'm not comfortable riding in the street. I am very close to the parked cars, and other cars driving past me make me nervous."

I glanced up at Clark Street just as a bus sped by. What was I thinking? Many adults don't like to ride through the busy part of town to the south of us. How could I expect him to do it? I had been lulled into complacency. The usual things that scared kids, that terrified me as a kid and a little still even as an adult, did not faze Ethan. Wicked witches? Flying monkeys? Werewolves? Vampires? Zombies? Zero discernible effect. Never even a bad dream. That was fine when it was merely a matter of whether *The Wizard of Oz* was too scary. The past couple of years I had become increasingly concerned that he was too fearless for his own good. Yet here I was pressing him into something that was potentially dangerous, simply because I clung to my vision of the summer. The vision thing got me every time. I was grateful he had the courage to express his apprehension to me.

He pressed himself to my side with his arms around my waist when I told him we would continue riding on the sidewalks until he was ready.

I did Pilates on my own, rather poorly, gained a little weight, and accomplished none of my goals for the summer. Instead, we had more time for happy hours at the beach, playdates, and outings with friends. Even the rainy days were a blast once we discovered the movie theater near us had a full bar.

"This is a dream summer," Ethan had said after yet another day with his friends, and I had to agree with him.

That was a sea change long in the making. Before Ethan was born, I had tried to control every aspect of my day because I assumed my life would fall apart without sufficient exercise, mental stimulation, and socializing. When I took on his all-encompassing medical care, I felt like I had crossed the "here be dragons" line on my life map. I didn't know what to expect. While there were many moments of pain and anguish, I gradually found ways to splice in tiny bits of what I wanted into our day together. My new baseline—getting nothing that I wanted—made the occasional moments for myself a cause for celebration.

Though my life had definitely been more exciting before, I much preferred the "here be dragons" side of the line. Studying abroad, interesting friends, great parties—all of that was hard to give up. Yet living in a love-filled cocoon with Janet and the kids eased the longing for my past life to the point where I didn't even think about it much anymore. Aristotle argued that happiness is an activity of virtue. Maybe the old guy was on to something. The previous year, I had declined an invitation to headline a conference devoted to a book I had translated and edited because I did not want to be away from home so soon after Penelope had arrived from China. That never would have happened ten years earlier. Not thinking exclusively of myself the past nine-plus years enabled me to rise above the under-current of dissatisfaction that had always tainted the good times before. Caring for others had made me happy.

Perhaps it also had made me phase shift–free. After Ethan was born, Janet said that I was good in a crisis, because responding to them took all my energy and completely occupied my mind. Yet that alone couldn't account for it. My elaborate pre-kid self-care regimen also gave me direction and purpose, but my brain waves still went out of sync every so often. I couldn't help but think that the difference was all the love I'd felt the last ten years, not only for my extended family but also for other kids, parents, teachers, doctors, nurses, friends, and neighbors. This love was like a magnetic field that held everything together for me regardless of the circumstances.

I could not explain how it worked, this love-induced neurological effect, nor could I account for how Ethan's hand taking my finger that first day in the NICU briefly calmed the internal electrical storms that had plagued me for much of my life. I was grateful then to have had that blissful moment with him, just as I was delighted and reassured now to live within this love-powered safe zone. I was no longer apprehensive about the future.

My musings were called to an abrupt halt when Penelope called out, "Geeoorrge!" He had arrived back with the dress, which, unfortunately, was not to the lady's specifications.

Backpedaling a bit, George blurted out, "It is red, Penelope. I like red."

"But I want white, George," she responded, her arms folded across her chest.

This can't have a positive outcome. I said, "How 'bout having the groom dress in red, and the bride's dress can be white?"

"Okay," Penelope said, arms akimbo. George smiled broadly.

I checked on Ethan and his friends. They were in a large group of kids far from shore, laughing and talking in ankle-deep water. Ethan was nose to nose with Ali, the girl who'd chosen him for the square dance unit in gym class. There were many more girls than boys in his class, so there was some apprehension among the boys that they would not be picked. It must have been some dance. Not only did he put her picture on his wall in place of his previous crush, but her mom informed us Ethan had stopped correcting her spelling in the notes she passed him.

While I was setting up a snack for Penelope and George, Ethan and Theo plopped down beside me.

Theo said, "I hope we are in the same class. It's going to be interesting having two male teachers. Do you think it will be different?"

"Oh yeah," Ethan responded. "I bet we can turn our assignments in by folding them into paper airplanes and throwing them up front. Or maybe we can jump from desk to desk to turn them in."

"That would be great," Theo said, laughing loudly.

We were all a bit startled when a candy bar landed on Ethan's lap as someone called out from behind, "We love you, Ham I Am."

It was Casey, who worked with Ethan on the third-grade newspaper. Casey was the editor and Ethan the cartoonist. Ethan's "Ham I Am" series was a class favorite about food trying to escape from a refrigerator to avoid becoming part of dinner. The three of them huddled out of earshot, their excited chatter punctuated by laughter.

I gazed at the lake and thought about Theo's question regarding male teachers for the first time. A similar change was occurring in my own work environment.

For the first nine years as a stay-at-home dad, I had very few male colleagues. I knew from news reports that the number of men home full-time with kids had been on the rise for quite a while. But in my milieu at least, they were very rare. Theo's dad was the only other one, and he and his family had come to Ethan's school not too long ago. When Ethan was around four, there was another stay-at-home dad on the next block, but he moved with his family to another neighborhood after about a year. Now, after the Great Recession, there were noticeably more men home with their kids. Before I could speculate on what difference it might make for me, the boys returned, and Theo opened a new conversation topic.

"I think that school is a little too uptight," he said. "It would be great to shake things up a bit. Do you find it hard to sit still all day? I do."

"Oh, man," Ethan said. "Like you wouldn't believe. I want to stand up and run around sometimes. My leg is often shaking, I'm so antsy. They definitely need to loosen things up."

"Yeah," Theo said. "Instead of coming and going through the regular doors, maybe we could rappel up and down the outside walls."

"Even in winter?" Ethan added with a hopeful look.

"Especially in winter," Theo answered. "That would be much more of a challenge."

Ethan nodded with a big smile. "You guys live so far away, maybe this year you could be helicoptered to school. Then parachute down and land on the roof, do a roll, and brace yourselves against the little wall up top until you could cut the cords with a knife."

"That would be great," Theo said with a big smile, apparently giving the idea some real thought. "Maybe we could do that at recess this year."

"Why not?" Ethan asked, smiling.

I glanced at them wondering how much longer they would feel comfortable talking so freely around me. The consensus view among parents of Ethan's friends was that they had already begun their secret preadolescent lives.

When that day comes, I will certainly miss listening to them discuss their lives, but not because I want to monitor them. Ethan and his friends were very thoughtful and well-spoken for their age, or any age, really.

At their first sleepover at age eight, Janet overheard Theo say in a post-midnight conversation about religion, "People can be spiritual in many different ways."

As a parent, I was reassured Ethan would go through life surrounded by a diverse group of creative, fun-loving, thoughtful people. I also simply enjoyed hearing them talk.

Theo broke the silence. "It's interesting how friendships change as you get older. Things get easier in some ways and more difficult in others."

"Yeah," Ethan said. "When you are a little kid, you share many of the same interests."

Theo nodded and said, "At that age, everyone likes to run around at the playground, put on costumes, and play hide-and-seek."

"Exactly," Ethan affirmed. "But not everyone likes climbing trees or sports or art or computers. Wait," he said with mock seriousness as though he suddenly became aware of some terrible oversight. "Everyone likes computers."

"Maybe not," Theo added. "It is possible that some kid somewhere doesn't like computers. Unlikely, but possible."

They laughed and looked out at the lake.

"Really, though, Ethan," Theo continued, "I know exactly what you mean. Like, we have different interests. Jonathan and I play baseball, but you don't, and you write comic books, but we don't. Still, we are good friends. What brings us together, do you think?"

"We make each other laugh?" Ethan responded.

"That's for sure," Theo said with a big smile. "I have to admit, when I first came to NCA, I thought it was a little weird that you wore hearing aids. But then I got to know you, and I realized it isn't weird at all. It's actually cool."

I peeked over at Ethan to see if he was hurt by this news, but he seemed completely unfazed. After all these years, I still didn't know what went on in his head. My distinct impression, however, was that Ethan saw hearing loss as a practical problem.

On vacation once, for example, he said he wished he could have heard his "pool friend" better because he wasn't wearing his hearing aids in the water. He wasn't upset or bitter. It was more a statement of fact comparable to someone on a hike acknowledging they wore the wrong shoes for the terrain. Sometimes hearing loss made his life difficult, but it did not affect his self-image or feelings of self-worth. He certainly wasn't going to let it diminish his enjoyment of life. He was the fun master, after all.

"I'm glad we got to know each other," Ethan said matter-of-factly, adding with a smile, "We always have the greatest times together."

"Oh, man," Theo said, "like yeah, totally."

A group of kids ran across the hot sand before making dramatic leaps onto their towels. Ethan and Theo laughed and cheered, then hustled over to talk to them.

Listening to them, I marveled at Ethan's apparent lack of self-consciousness. Wearing braces on my legs as a kid was a constant source of embarrassment. No one made fun of me or thought less of me for it. But I couldn't get it off my mind. It colored everything I did. Learning later that I should not have been wearing them only made me even more resentful. Ethan had become an inspiration for me. When I started wearing unsightly orthotics a few years ago, I decided not to conceal them or be embarrassed about them. The true test would be if I ended up in braces again one day. I knew I could not match Ethan in terms of not letting a misfortune or disability darken my outlook. Who could? My great hope was I would not be consumed with self-pity and rage, as I was before.

Penelope's friend George left with his dad and his little brother.

Penelope sat in my lap and thumbed through a book. When visions of her sleeping quietly for an hour began dancing through my head like the proverbial sugarplums, I called the kids into shore. Their disappointment about leaving was mollified somewhat by the prospect of a playdate at our house.

After a couple of hours, all the kids except Augie had been picked up. Janet got home from work and went upstairs to pack for our trip to the beach in southwest Michigan. Penelope and I settled down on the couch in the basement to watch a movie together while the boys played behind us.

My attention flagged once the wizard turned the princess into a swan. Finished with my popcorn, I moved closer to Penelope in hopes of getting some of hers, when I overheard Ethan say, "Maybe they had hovercraft tanks like Transformers. They could change in an instant from a tank to a hovercraft and back again to a tank."

"They definitely only had conventional tanks in 1939," Augie deadpanned. "The Germans just made more effective use of them."

Augie moved several tanks to the left flank while Ethan added a medieval knight and a wizard to the battle scene. I was astonished when Augie positioned a dragon to counter them. Augie's interests, military history at that time, were a little out of the ordinary, as was his focus on them, which was unwavering, in fact, tractor-beam-like. Ethan enjoyed his quirkiness and was adept at getting him to think outside whatever box he was in at the moment.

"You know, Augie. It would be totally awesome if we all had hovercrafts. I could go to my friend Sean's house on my own, maybe even Theo's or yours, because I wouldn't have to cross any streets. I could fly above any overhanging branches or power lines."

"Not so high, though, that they would interfere with airplanes and helicopters," Augie cautioned. Ethan nodded while moving an oversized librarian action figure to counter some of Augie's troop movements, slyly pushing the button to activate its "amazing shushing action" feature before placing the wizard in front of the entire contingent. "How big would they be?" Augie asked.

"Mine would have two seats, kid size, and a small compartment for Legos and other stuff," Ethan answered.

"I would rather have a one-seater," Augie responded without explanation.

"They wouldn't have to have two seats," Ethan said. "They're Transformers. At the touch of a button, they could change from one seat to two and back again. People with wizard training might not even have to use buttons and onboard computers. They could use their wand instead."

"Could it change from a fighter plane to a heavy bomber or perhaps a seaplane?" Augie asked.

"See, that's the great thing," Ethan responded. "Each kid could customize their hovercraft. Even the colors could change instantly. When I'm taking Penelope somewhere, it could be pink. And when you are using it, it could be camouflaged and have military insignias. Since they are Transformers, maybe when you aren't using them, they could shrink down and be kept in those little containers like Pokémons. Then our parents couldn't complain about them cluttering up the house. In fact, you wouldn't even need one of your own. There could be stations throughout the city where you could pick one up to use for a particular purpose and then return it. I could zip over to Theo and Eden's, drop it off, and pick up another to come home later. My dad always laughs about Percy Jackson and his friends needing a ride from their moms in order to save the world. We might not be saving the world, but we will save our parents the trouble of driving us around."

"Well, okay," Augie answered, apparently finally sold on the idea, "as long as you can customize them like you said."

The movie ended, Janet took Penelope upstairs to get ready for bed, and the boys settled in the tent on the upstairs deck. Penelope joined them early in the evening, only to return to our room shortly after midnight.

In the morning, I stepped out on the porch, instinctively propping the door open with my right foot to let our cats scurry past me to their food bowls. Today, though, there was no mad rush inside. In uncharacteristic fashion, Snuggles remained sitting on the sidewalk looking back and forth, perhaps, like me, expecting Sylvester to come hustling up for breakfast.

Sylvester had met an ignoble end the week before. Someone brought his dog on the porch right up to where Sylvester sat. Feeling threatened in the very innermost portion of his territory, the former feline master of the neighborhood jumped on top of the dog and sprang over to bite the dog's owner on the leg before running out to the curb, where he keeled over, dead. We were all still in shock, especially Ethan.

I sat down on the swing with the laptop and opened a video Ethan's piano teacher Lauren had sent. Two days before, I had forgotten Ethan had a piano lesson and had to call him in from down the street, where he and his friend George were playing in the sprinkler with the neighbor kids. Still in his swimsuit and sopping wet, Ethan hunched over the keys with a huge frown. He perked up, though, after a few minutes, closing by playing his own composition, Prelude in A Minor. Lately he had been hurrying through it so he could get out to play more. This time he did it at the proper speed, and she happened to record it.

"Did you get that?" he had asked her with a sly smile.

I played the video. "What a haunting piece," I whispered. Ethan had told Lauren he preferred the minor keys, which surprised me given what a sunny disposition he had. Janet, though, thought he had seemed sad over the summer. *Maybe he was giving expression to that through his music.* Ethan came out on the porch and sat down next to me.

"Do you think Snuggles is looking for Sylvester?" he asked.

"Yes, I think so. She must be lonely without him."

After a pause, he said, "It is lonely without him. I wish he would come jump up on my lap and let me pet him."

"Yeah," I said with a sigh, "he was a great cat. One of a kind."

"I love Snuggles," he said sadly, "but it's not the same with her as it was with Sylvester. She's not as affectionate as Sylvester was."

"That's true," I said. "And he was definitely your cat. He loved you above all."

Actually, Sylvester loved his food bowl above all, though Ethan, who showered him with love, was a very close second.

The voices of kids playing down the block caught our attention. "Can I go play with Emmitt and Joe?"

"What about Augie?" I asked. "You can't just abandon him."

"I'm not," he said. "He's downstairs setting up the Battle of the Bulge."

"Augie said yesterday it is also known as the 'Ardennes Counteroffensive.' Can't we stick to that?" I asked hopefully, self-conscious about my summer weight gain.

Ethan shrugged his shoulders, saying, "Sure."

I looked down the street and saw parents carrying bags out to cars, suggesting he would not be gone long. I nodded, and he jumped up and ran down the block letting out his distinctive yell. A moment later, Ethan and a bunch of kids, all with scarves tied around their foreheads, ran past our house, circled a neighbor's garden, and ran back down the block.

Ethan returned about half an hour later, followed in short order by Sean's older sister Catherine. That was my cue to begin packing the car. I had learned a valuable lesson in trip preparation earlier in the summer. Ethan, Penelope, and I visited Grandma while Janet was on a business trip. Thankfully, Cousin Grace happened to be visiting too. Though much older, she was happy to spend countless hours with them playing games, reading, and telling stories. They were so sated with play that they didn't whine a bit on the return trip. My takeaway? Set up a sleepover for Ethan and hire beloved Catherine to play with Penelope before any major road trip.

I closed the trunk and went inside to check on the kids. Ethan and Penelope were now playing the Wii with Catherine watching on the couch and Augie crouched over an elaborate battle scene behind her on the floor. Penelope moved her arm like she was rolling a bowling ball.

"What fun," I said, feeling a bit like Rip Van Winkle, who had awoken from a twenty-year slumber to find the world transformed. They all nodded without looking away from the screen.

Ethan had gotten the Wii from their Aunt Joan about a month before as an early birthday present. He was beside himself with excitement about it. We had told him he could get video games when he was twelve years old, which then was still a little over two years away. He had wanted video games so badly that he made a fake game console out of cardboard.

"However can I thank you?" he said to Joan when she gave him the news.

Shortly before noon, we all piled into the car, dropped Catherine off, and began winding our way through the city to Augie's house in Humboldt Park. Gentrification was less advanced in that part of the city. The businesses and public spaces didn't have the homogenous, airbrushed quality of the glitzier precincts on the city's North Side. The sidewalks were full of people enjoying a leisurely Saturday. It was charming to see kids talk excitedly with their parents, siblings, and friends as they made their way by foot or on all manner of conveyances.

The scene was like a public service announcement for family life that made me aware of how much I still had to learn about parenting. An incident the previous week came to mind. Janet's brain integration study group was meeting downstairs while I tried to put Penelope to bed. She wanted her mom and was not budging. I became increasingly anxious about the scene she was creating, worried about the impression I imagined it was making on the crowd downstairs. They might think that I was a fumble-fingered dad with no experience with childcare, that Penelope didn't like me, or that I was an abusive parent. Penelope became more agitated as I became more annoyed. Ethan tried to distract her, but I took it the wrong way, thinking he was going to get her more excited, not settle her down.

"It's not the time for that now," I snapped, nudging him in the side with my elbow. He ran crying back to the TV room and crouched in my closet. I apologized to him, and he came out and helped me put Penelope to bed.

We talked about it the next day. He explained the elaborate plan he had wanted to use to help ease Penelope into sleep. I was genuinely impressed by the scheme and was sure it would have worked, if only I had given him the opportunity to try it. I told him that I loved his idea and promised that next time I would follow his lead.

I looked at him in the rearview mirror, grateful for all the time we had spent together over the summer. It reminded me of how close we'd been when he was little. I knew that as he became more distant as an adolescent, I would remember this summer fondly, not just because we had so much fun together but also because we learned to talk with one another about our feelings.

We dropped Augie off. While Janet and Penelope went to a coffee shop across the street, Ethan and I returned to the car, where he read while I consulted a map. After I put the map away, I glanced back at him. How ironic it was that a nine-year-old boy was helping his fifty-two-year-old father with his emotional development. Maybe with Ethan as my mentor, there was hope for me after all.

23 Thanks for the Memories

JANET AND I SAT in our kitchen with our friend Carol several days after Ethan's funeral. The outside world still felt alien and inhospitable then. Even the thought of sitting in the backyard was unsettling.

"It's really quite beautiful," I said of our garden as if I were commenting on a painting, not something we ourselves could experience.

"You know, I have light memories," Carol said. "The angle and intensity of light at different times of year call forth specific memories for me."

Two weeks later, standing on my little brother Chris's back deck in Omaha, the day after what would have been Ethan's tenth birthday, I watched shadows cast by the late afternoon sun, imagining them as elongated shade people in different postures, some erect, others bent over something. If Carol was right, and I believed she was, the light then, still bright, though a little less direct than in mid-August when Ethan died, should have reminded me of the time after Ethan's birth. Yet I could not remember it. The only memory I had of him was of the two of us drowning together. Ten years of laughter and love amidst pain and suffering, and that's all I could remember.

Chris came out of the house with Penelope and his two sons, Gus and Harrison, trailing close behind him. They smiled at me as they ran off the deck and up to the fence on the west side of the yard. There was a bit of jostling for position before they plopped onto the ground and rolled one after another down the hill, piling up together at the bottom with peals of laughter. Soon, they were up and down the slide on the east side of the yard and chasing one another around the big pine tree near the back end.

Watching them was like being a scientist studying another species. I doubted I would be able to give myself over to play or feel joy ever again. We'd come to Chris and Jeannie's partly because we had trouble being alone once family and friends went back to their lives after a couple of weeks of constantly being at our side. There was also the sense that we might not make it. The loss being impossible to bear, one day we might walk into the lake and not return. We wanted to be sure Penelope would find a loving home.

Janet joined me on the porch. She wrapped her arms around my waist and leaned her head against mine while we watched Chris and the kids scamper past us into the house.

Once they were inside, Janet said, "I want to go back to the beach and say a few prayers."

Stunned, I just stared back at her while my mind raced. After Ethan died, I told her that taking care of her and Ethan had changed my life and taking care of Penelope and her would save my life, so she could ask me anything, and I would do it. But that? I could not return to the beach because I'd never left it. Images of the waves overtaking us and the two of us sinking together played in my head like a video set on a continuous feedback loop.

She hugged me. Perhaps sensing my withdrawal, she gave me a moment to recover. I took a deep breath and squeaked, "Okay."

We separated and pivoted toward the yard like figures in a clock-tower glockenspiel performance. Janet broke the silence.

"At Ethan's funeral, Alexander said he was able to find Ethan's body because Buddhist meditation enabled him to concentrate on the movement of the water currents and where they would have carried him."

I squeezed my eyes shut and shook my head at the image of Ruth carrying Ethan's lifeless body to shore. I was frozen in place then when I noticed that his beautiful face was blue like my hands and feet were when I was pulled out of the water.

Feeling Janet pressed against me, I turned toward her and said, "Right before Ethan and I went in the water, I was reading a section in *The Iliad* about the death of Zeus's son Sarpedon. Zeus agreed to allow him to die in the Trojan War, as was his fate, if Apollo promised to spirit his body away, so that he could have a proper burial. Then, a guy with a Greek name, Alexander, meaning 'defender of the people,' found Ethan when no one else could. It is like one god took him from us, and a rival god brought him back. So, he just heard about a missing child on the radio and came down to help?"

"Yes," she said. "Lucky for us. Sometimes drowning victims are never found. It was such a gift being able to say goodbye to him. I am grateful to the EMTs for massaging his heart, even though they knew he was already gone. It brought back his natural color. He looked like his beautiful self, just in a deep sleep, when I kissed him goodbye."

I sighed and put my arm around her shoulder. After a long pause, she said, "Alexander also told me that *The Tibetan Book of Living and Dying* helped him after his mother died. The Tibetans believe that one relives their death each week to the day for the next seven weeks and that you can help them get through it with prayers and meditation. If we leave tomorrow, we can go to the beach Monday on week four."

"Okay," I said, adding, "good idea" in a feeble effort to be supportive, though I was really filled with trepidation.

Janet kissed me on the cheek and went back inside. I stared back into the yard and thought about how impressive it was that she could think so clearly and calmly. It was not that she was less affected by Ethan's death. On the contrary, she simply processed her grief differently than I did, which produced an informal division of labor between us. Grief for me was very emotive and expressive. Tears shot from my eyes like from a water cannon. I had very little control over it. Janet was more reflective.

Missy's mom, Babette, had a son who'd died fifteen years before Ethan. She told Janet though her relationship with the beautiful physical Ethan was over, she was beginning her relationship with him in his spiritual form. When she was not cuddling with Penelope or comforting friends and family, she was reading everything she could get her hands on about spirituality and the afterlife.

"I am a heaven person now," Janet said to me a few days after Ethan's funeral, determined to cultivate her spiritual relationship with him the best she could.

I wished her luck. I would have been happy to have had just one memory of him besides that of our last few moments together underwater. Nothing could shake the hold that those soul-crushing images had on me. Even reading through some of my four thousand pages of notes of our time together did not loosen their grip on me. It was like I was reading about someone else entirely. I felt completely disconnected from him and was becoming resigned to spending every waking moment of the rest of my life at the beach drowning with him. If saying a few prayers there made her feel better, I would go along with it.

Thank God for Al Keating, a stranger who had quickly become an intimate friend. Though I had no recollection of him, he had pulled me from the water after he had swum out to try to save Ethan. I had assumed that I could not recall how I reached the surface because I could not face the possibility that I sacrificed Ethan to save myself. As people tried to console me by saying that I had done everything I could to save him, I expected to hear the tell-tale heart beating in the background.

"Don't you know I killed him!" I wanted to scream.

Al could not explain how I survived. But he was with us in the time between me struggling to keep Ethan above the water and then me with him underwater trying frantically to carry him to the surface. Sharing with us what happened during my personal bardo silenced the tell-tale heart.

A week after Ethan's funeral, I sat at the bottom of the stairs leading from our front parlor to the second story, waiting for Al and his wife, Rose, to arrive, tormented by the thought that maybe I was just not strong enough to save Ethan. Though an excellent swimmer with lifeguard training and in great physical condition, I had recently recovered from a reaggravated shoulder injury. I had received a clean bill of health and had resumed a full training regimen some time before. But maybe I was not 100 percent. More time in the gym may have made a difference. And there was the whole petite thing. Was I simply not big enough to get him to the surface? I was at least twenty pounds lighter, however, when I easily carried a two-hundred-pound lifeguard instructor from the bottom of the pool to safety. Of course, that was over thirty years before. Though I looked young for my age by most accounts, aging was not a hoax. I was older. Perhaps a younger, larger, and/or stronger person would have succeeded where I failed.

A knock at the door mercifully released me from my troubled musings. A figure almost completely filled the entryway. It was Al, a gentle giant of a man, tall, broad-shouldered, and well muscled from regular weight training, my age, though also very youthful.

Setting everyone up with coffee, tea, water, and some cookies and fruit, we settled into the front parlor. Al and Rose sat on the couch in front of the floor-to-ceiling bookshelves. Their heads were framed by photos, kid's artwork, and kooky knickknacks that filled the mid-level shelves. Janet settled into the glider chair to their right after depositing a pile of unopened mail on the floor. I sat on the bottom step of the staircase to the second floor across from Al and Rose.

We chatted amiably about their backgrounds, how they met, their work, and their kids. They both had very gentle demeanors and seemed sad, which I had at first assumed was on our behalf. But very quickly it struck me that their sadness was deeper than sympathy for our loss, and more than an aftereffect of the trauma Al experienced trying to save Ethan.

They, too, had lost a child. Their daughter, Valerie, had died at twenty-five not quite two years before Ethan. She had cerebral palsy and lived at home with them. Though she never spoke, they developed unconventional ways of communicating with one another. They were both devastated by her passing. That terrible day when Ethan died was the first time after Valerie's death that Al had ventured to the beach from their vacation home nearby.

Janet and I were both astonished and outraged when they related that Al's grief counselor had told him he should be "over it" after a year. We could not imagine ever recovering from the loss of Ethan. That was our first experience with how grief separates you from everyone else. Even some grief counselors do not fully understand that you are disabled and will never fully recover. Our sadness about Ethan formed a ring around Janet and me that marked us off from nongrieving people. While they shared their own grief, the ring expanded to include them as well. It seemed as though we had known each other forever.

After a long pause, Al said that he was saying a prayer of gratitude for the beauty of the surf when he noticed Ethan and I struggling in the water. He asked several bystanders if they thought we were in trouble. They thought we were just playing.

"You can't blame them," Janet interjected. "I've read that is a common reaction of witnesses to people drowning. They don't appear much different from those around them."

"Yes, I can see how they could think that," Al said. "But I still sensed something was not right. So I looked around for something like a life ring. But there was only a boogie board. I entered the surf, but the board was too light and got blown away by the waves immediately. So I swam out and took Ethan from you."

"It was so brave of you to risk your life to try to save our darling boy. We are both very grateful," I said, trying to remember Al, but only drawing a blank.

"And when you were still grieving the loss of your own daughter," Janet added, prompting me to cry a little.

"Well, thank you," Al said. "I just couldn't stand by and do nothing. I took Ethan, but the waves were too powerful. I was taking on water and coughing a lot. I felt like I was drowning. I told Ethan he had to hold onto me with both hands, so that I could use both of my hands to swim back to shore."

Al paused for a moment, tears welling up in his eyes. He collected himself and said, "Ethan's arms went limp. I think he died then."

I burst into tears and almost slid off the step, I shook so violently. With a quavering voice, I said, "I am so grateful that he died in the arms of such a loving man. I was so worried," I continued with heaving sobs, "that he died alone, and that I had abandoned him."

"No, no, you did not abandon him," Al said reassuringly. "When I passed Ethan back to you, all three of us went under. That's when

I saw the light. I felt strongly that it was not my time. With a surge of adrenaline, I made it to the surface. It was very hard swimming back to shore. I think it must have taken me five minutes. I coughed up a bunch of water and asked bystanders if they had seen you. They said that only I came back up. It was another five minutes before you surfaced."

Janet called to me from an upstairs window. I was so immersed in the memory of talking with Al that I was a little disoriented at first. It was like the Janet-in-the-memory was speaking to me.

"Penelope is going to bed," the present-moment Janet repeated. Still a little shaky, I began the trek to the upstairs bedroom.

I entered to find Chris jumping on their king-sized bed with the kids, playing a game Ethan loved so much, karate-chop master, where Chris dove toward them and made fake chopping motions on their backs. They were all laughing uncontrollably and falling from side to side.

After a debriefing about the results of the karate-chop master game, Penelope went to sleep, and the boys drifted off to the basement to watch a movie. Janet and I joined Chris and Jeannie in the living room, with Jeannie and Janet sitting on a very comfy new couch. Chris and I sat in chairs that had been passed down from our maternal grandparents, which I'd thought were very uncomfortable when I sat on them as a kid. They had definitely not mellowed with age. The cushions were still hard, and they were contoured such that you could never quite settle into them without feeling a pain somewhere—your back, side, buttocks. I shifted around trying to get comfortable to no avail.

Chris keeping all this stuff had always puzzled me. I had very vivid memories of my childhood. I could call up people's faces in my mind's eye very easily, remember features of buildings, recall events, almost as though I were there. Of course, we had many photos of Ethan and Penelope, quite a few of our time together before kids as well. Most of them were in a file cabinet, completely unorganized. Chris's front room, by contrast, was like a photo gallery. There were the usual photos of his wife and kids, but also other photos of parents, grandparents, extended families, even friends and neighbors from our childhood.

I wandered over to gaze at the photos while the three of them talked, partly to get some relief from the heirlooms from hell but also because I was starting to understand why Chris's house was like a family museum. My photographic memory failed me when it came to Ethan. I needed things—other people, photos, memorabilia, familiar places—to remind me of him, what he was like, what he meant to me. Chris was devastated when our mom died shortly before his twenty-first birthday, and again when our dad died fourteen years later. He clung to bits and pieces of connections lost, longing to feel them in his life. Chris helped me feel connected to Ethan through his playful spirit. I wished I could have helped him more with his feeling of loss.

I rejoined the group, though this time on the floor. We shared stories about our families as we drank wine, beer, and soda and munched on chips and popcorn till well after midnight. We finally parted with long hugs and considerable tears. Janet and I slept in Chris and Jeannie's bedroom, which they let us use while they slept on cots in their boys' rooms. Janet climbed into bed with Penelope and fell asleep. I plopped down on the carpeted floor by the bay window.

I desperately wanted to sleep too. The pain of Ethan's loss was so intense that every day I felt like I had a screw drilled into my forehead. After spending the entire day trying to get the screw out,

I collapsed into a fretful sleep, which granted me temporary relief from the torment.

With a return to the beach looming, I did not even have a brief respite. The two of us, the screw and I, kept a silent vigil all night. I can't say how it passed the time. I was consumed with anguished thoughts about that last terrible day, the struggle in the water, Ethan's lifeless body, what we should have done, and how we might have saved him.

The sun rose, filling the room with brilliant, warm yellow light. Birds chirped outside the window. Janet and Penelope were still asleep.

Gazing out the window at the beautiful sunshine, I sighed with the thought that Ethan had desperately wanted to go swimming that day, and he'd wanted to do it with me. I cried feeling grateful that I was with him when he died. "We are bonded, favorite guy, in life as well as death," I whispered, closing my eyes again with the intention of getting up.

Instead, I was standing at the bottom of the stairs in the front parlor of our house in Chicago. I gazed up the staircase and began climbing. The old wood creaked with each footfall. My legs were stiff for the first couple of steps but quickly loosened up. I watched my thighs rise and lower, feeling a little surprised by the motion. I became so absorbed in their movement that I lost my balance and tipped to the left. Grasping the handrail to right myself, the sideways momentum caused me to slam my elbow hard against the wall. I felt a sharp pain and stopped to rub it before continuing up the stairs. I shook my elbow again before completing the last few steps.

Standing at the top of the stairs, I glanced left toward our bedroom and right toward the back room, not aware that I was looking for anything in particular. Then, I noticed the light on in Ethan's room. What was visible from the hallway appeared neat and tidy, quite a contrast to the creative chaos Ethan cultivated in his space. Aleta stayed in his room after he had died. Not as nimble as Ethan, who could dance through the clutter with ease, she needed a bit more floor space, so she put his books in the built-in bookshelf that spanned much of one wall and found places for some of his art supplies, careful to leave most of the room in the uniquely disordered state that made it so Ethan.

I walked up to the entryway and surveyed the room. Before he died, he had bunk beds flush to the wall on the right side. We had planned for some time to take them apart but never got around to it. Uncle Matt and Cousin Joe did it the day after his funeral, leaving one single bed against the wall and moving the other into the finished attic.

The room was exactly as it was when we left Chicago for Omaha except for one thing. Ethan was sleeping in the single bed with his back to me. He was a little guy, however, perhaps four or five years old, not the tall, lanky preteen he was becoming. His legs were curled up with the lower portions perpendicular to the upper thighs, almost like he was preparing to do a twist in a yoga class. He had the slightly oversized, somewhat square head of kids of kindergarten age, and his hair was also blonder and shorter than it was at the time of his death. I watched him for a moment before saying, "Ahhh . . . there you are."

I opened my eyes to find myself back in Chris and Jeannie's bedroom. Bolting upright, I shook my head in disbelief. "What the fuck was that?"

I scanned the room. Janet and Penelope remained blissfully asleep. The birds still chirped on the windowsill. I was charmed by the way they hopped up and down and from side to side as they faced one another singing, much as Ethan and his friends had jumped on and off the benches in front of our house, talking excitedly and laughing as they waited for me to take them to the water park on the first day of summer vacation. I had stood on the porch in awe of all the boy energy. I had almost expected to see sparks flying off their heads.

I glanced back at the window, disappointed the little birds were gone. The sun shining on my face soothed me. I had a very peaceful feeling, calm and untroubled, much like how I'd felt just after Ethan took my finger in the NICU on his first day. *Adieu, screw!*

I closed my eyes, hoping to sleep. Ethan's face appeared instead. The image was from an afternoon a couple of weeks before he died after we'd made a premature exit from basketball camp. I knew he was especially tired after an outing at Millennium Park the day before with his friends and Penelope, so I suggested he skip.

"No pro scouts will be there today, buddy."

He shook his head, kissed Penelope on her forehead, and took a place in the stands to wait for the coaches to call him. I was a little surprised by his response. He didn't care about basketball all that much. However, he did want to be a good teammate. Maybe that was it. The simple fact was I didn't know why he insisted on staying. In contrast to me, he wasn't very expressive about his feelings, leaving me only to guess about his motivations.

But there he was, his arms crossed, tired. I decided to ask him again. Once more, he shook his head. Penelope and I left. Thinking he might change his mind, however, we waited by the exit, an area not visible to him in the stands but in sight of kids on the court, who had already been called by the coaches. Those kids watched us intently over the shoulders of the coaches, perhaps sensing what was afoot and longing to leave themselves. A few seconds later, Ethan came tearing around the corner, almost knocking us over when he barreled into us.

"Can we still go?" he asked hopefully, an arm around Penelope's shoulder.

"I'm glad you decided to come with us, Ethan," I said as we walked toward the car. "I was hoping we could go play some miniature golf."

"Oh, man, would I love that," he said, giving me a little bump on my shoulder with the side of his head, much like the way our cats rub against our legs when we feed them.

Penelope served as ball spotter and scout, finding our balls before running ahead to explore the next hole. Ethan took frequent breaks to poke around with her and excitedly pointed out unique features of the course layout, pretending not to know where she had hidden herself behind various nooks and crannies. When not goofing around with Penelope, he played the course with a surprising level of seriousness. I was pleased he had progressed past the little kids' style of play of awkwardly pushing the ball toward the hole. He lined up his putts and worked deliberately around obstacles. We talked about the summer, his friends, the books he was reading, all the while laughing about the bizarre holes and the predicaments in which we found ourselves.

After mini golf, lunch, and a stop at the big used bookstore on Lincoln Avenue, we drove up Racine toward home. As we passed the quirky Wisconsin bar south of Belmont, Penelope pointed frantically at the giant moose statue on the patio and wanted to stop. She and I had spent many hours there playing arcade games and watching the fish in the giant tank up front while Ethan was in karate class nearby. Ethan had said he wanted to go there with us, so I pulled over and we made our way inside with an armful of used books.

Finding a spot on the patio next to the moose, Penelope devoted herself to a huge bowl of popcorn, and Ethan read. I sat there, lost in thought about how the rest of the day would go. I looked up after a while to find Ethan smiling at me.

"Thanks for today, Dad," he said. "It was a great time."

"It was, indeed," I whispered, sitting up with a smile while I savored the image of his beautiful face.

I took a deep breath and sighed, grateful the memories of Ethan had returned. I went downstairs to see if Chris wanted to go for a bike ride, but he was gone. Deciding to go on my own, I pulled Janet's new foldable bike out of our trunk. It was a design marvel, folding up into a little triangle about three feet long, two feet high, and a foot and half wide. Rooting around in the car for the instructions, I recalled Janet's story about learning how to open and close it with Ethan. After watching the demo at the bike shop, she reluctantly reached down to try, only to find Ethan's hands already there. He had effortlessly opened it for her.

After getting the bike open and stowing the instructions, I rode down the street. With its tiny wheels and exaggeratedly long handlebar and seat stems, I felt like a bear on a bike in the circus. The undersized wheels wobbled on the rough pavement as I went through a deserted four-way stop at the bottom of the hill and started up a very steep incline. Descending again, the bike shook as I picked up speed. I felt like I was with Ethan again on the old roller coasters we'd ridden while Janet was in China picking up Penelope two years before.

I crossed a very wide street with large medians and coasted along a short, flat stretch with a used car lot on one side of the street and a couple of plain brick apartment buildings on the other. "Get in character," I whispered as I started up a long, dauntingly steep hill. After passing a few dilapidated houses on both sides of the street, I was startled by a barking dog that jumped out from behind a car, straining at the leash. As I neared the summit, pedaling slowly with considerable effort, a couple of kids on big tricycles careened down the street and waved at me, laughing and smiling.

Reaching the top of the hill, out of breath, I pulled over to see what became of the kids. Far down the block, they turned suddenly, toppling over onto the sidewalk. Laughing uncontrollably, they stumbled a bit side to side before trudging up the hill again. One of them stopped. Our eyes locked. He smiled and waved at me before hurrying to catch up with his friend.

I watched them enter a house together, then gazed back down the hill, struck by how beautiful it all was. The same tacky used car lot, drab apartment buildings, run-down houses, everything the same, and yet now breathtaking, like a majestic mountain valley, not an ordinary city street. I stood, amazed, as a soothing warmth spread throughout my tired, aching body, and with it the realization that in that moment I was viewing the world through Ethan's eyes, seeing beauty everywhere.

Tears ran down my cheeks as I got on the bike and continued on toward the next hill, wishing the moment would never end.

Afterword:
Goodbye Letter to Ethan

DEAR ETHAN,

We, the members of the Committee for Stating the Obvious, affirm unequivocally: you are the Fun Master. We are your devoted pupils. Never before has there been such an enjoyable course of study. In fact, we didn't even object to the homework. Our only complaint is our Fun Academy closed unexpectedly without any prospect of reopening. And we are left to soldier on as best we can without our guiding light.

And lack of fun is not a bourgeois problem. You would understand this. It's serious and we desperately need your help. You always made us laugh. Nothing will replace your big, throaty cackle or your ingenious schemes. So come back to us please, Ethan.

You humble and inspire us every day. You experienced a lifetime of troubles in your first week, and that was just the beginning. Did that ever diminish the joy that radiated from your impossibly beautiful blue eyes? Not for a second. We can only feel awe in the presence of such a spirit.

Ethan, we miss you for so many reasons. But your unfailing kindness is perhaps your most remarkable quality. You taught us to understand people, to see them for what they are, good and bad, and yet still love them. This quality meant so much to us. How wonderful for your little sister Penelope to have a big brother who loved her so much and was willing to share his life (not to mention his tent) with her, often on her terms. As she put it: "My gēgē loves me." Thank you for sharing so much love with us. How will we go on without you?

Apparently, we could go on and on about you. But we'll stop here. We will always remember you, honor you, and emulate you (failingly). Mostly, though, we miss you.

You are the light of our lives.

With hearts bursting with love for you,

Your devoted parents and your loving mei mei.

St. Gertrude Parish Bulletin,
August 18, 2010

Acknowledgments

IT IS SAID THAT it takes a village. In my case, it's more like a medium-sized city.

My mother-in-law, Aleta Smith, encouraged me to jot down some of my stories about my unlikely stint as a stay-at-home dad. The result was over four thousand pages of notes, transcribed by Joan Batchen, which provided much of the material for the book.

Fellow students and instructors at the Story Studio and at the University of Chicago, members of the Edgewater Writers, Dark Stuff, and Write Now writing groups, and colleagues at the Writers WorkSpace all helped me pivot from scholarly writing to creative nonfiction. Many people guided me as I honed my writing skills. I am especially grateful for the advice and encouragement of Elisabeth Bayley, Brendan Butkus, Neil Christiansen, Elizabeth Coughlan, Jim Crilly, Ben Durham, Clarence Ford, Kristin Gourlay, Liz Granger, Maegan Gwaltney, Laurie Hasbrook, Margo Hines, David Ingram, Nadine Kenney Johnstone, Alice Jun, John Neafsey, Thomas Pace, Kim Peek, Marcia Pradzinski, Patrick Reardon, Sarah Terez Rosenblum, Peggy Shinner, Grace Smith, Rachal Steele, Michael Steeves, Megan Stielstra, Mary-Lisa Sullivan, Anna Valentine, Anita Vijayakumar, and Allison K. Williams.

I am also indebted to Brooke Warner and SparkPress for taking a chance on a guy with a story to tell but without a platform to match.

Early on, my wife Janet said I should try to make people laugh. I can't say if I succeeded. I'm grateful to her, our daughter Penelope, and countless others who kept *me* laughing much of the time I spent writing this book. I couldn't have completed it without their wit and good cheer.

About the Author

© Zoe McKenzie Photography

JEFF SEITZER WAS AN expert on the care of the self, himself in particular, before he unexpectedly became a stay-at-home dad concerned with other people's needs. Accounts of his on-the-job training in parenting have appeared in newspapers, magazines, and literary journals such as the *Omaha World-Herald, Hippocampus, Brevity Nonfiction Blog, CMTA Report,* and *Adoptive Families.* An award-winning teacher, he is also the author of a number of books and articles on law and philosophy. Born and raised in Omaha, Nebraska, he now lives with his family in Chicago, where he teaches philosophy and religion at Roosevelt University.

SELECTED TITLES FROM SPARKPRESS

SparkPress is an independent boutique publisher delivering high-quality, entertaining, and engaging content that enhances readers' lives, with a special focus on female-driven work. www.gosparkpress.com

Engineering a Life: A Memoir, Krishan K. Bedi. $16.95, 978-1-943006-43-4
A memoir of Krishan Bedi's experiences as a young Indian man in the South in the 1960s, this is a story of one man's perseverance and determination to create the life he'd always dreamed for himself and his family, despite his options seeming anything but limitless.

Mission Afghanistan: An Army Doctor's Memoir, Elie Cohen, translation by Jessica Levine. $16.95, 978-1-943006-65-6
Decades after evading conscription as a young man, Franco-British doctor Elie Paul Cohen is offered a deal by the French Army: he can settle his accounts by becoming a military doctor and serving at Camp Bastion in Afghanistan.

Roots and Wings: Ten Lessons of Motherhood that Helped Me Create and Run a Company, Margery Kraus with Phyllis Piano
$16.95, 978-1-68463-024-0
Margery Kraus, a trailblazing corporate and public affairs professional who became a mother at twenty-one, shares ten lessons from motherhood and leadership that enabled her to create, run, and grow a global company. Her inspiring story of crashing through barriers as she took on increasingly challenging opportunities will have women of all ages cheering.

Even if Your Heart Would Listen: Losing My Daughter to Heroin, Elise Schiller. $16.95, 978-1-68463-008-0
In January of 2014, Elise Schiller's daughter, Giana Natali, died of a heroin overdose. *Even if Your Heart Would Listen* is a memoir about Giana's illness and death and its impact on her family—especially her mother—as well as a close examination and critique of the treatment she received from health care practitioners while she was struggling to get well.